As Natural As Breathing: Being Intuitive

Author: Vanessa F. Hurst, ms

Wildefyr Press
Louisville, Kentucky

Wildefyr Press
Louisville, KY 40242

Published in 2020
Printed in the USA

ISBN-10: 0-9908091-6-1
ISBN-13: 978-0-9908091-6-6

This book is a way station on a journey of intuitive understand that began many years ago. I could not have written this book without my community. Thanks to my editor, Marlene, and my beta readers, Nicci, Lori, and Barbara. To Merlin, who is both an intuitive sounding board and intuitive voice, for illustrating this book. To the students who have learned from and taught me. To the friends who share their intuition while encouraging me to listen to mine. To Peggy, Mary, Retha, and countless others who supported me during the writing of this book. In gratitude and with love, Vanessa

Table of Contents

Foreword

For many decades I have traveled along the intuitive awareness continuum. Since I was a small child, I knew things that I should not know. Even then, I was connected to my intuition. In time, I learned to be silent about what I knew, what I saw until I stopped consciously acknowledging my intuition.

But, there was encouragement on this journey. Books would appear from the most remarkable sources — a book on numerology from a small-town dime store. Jonathan Livingston Seagull as a Confirmation gift. While my mother was both intuitively gifted and a Catholic with a strong devotion to Mary, she did not understand how connected she was to her intuition. She regularly had premonitions and would see people after they had died. Mom followed those intuitive hunches and often prayed for people who were deceased.

When I began teaching almost a quarter of a century ago, a student reminded me that I needed to understand the how and why behind my intuitive abilities if I was going to share them. This began my journey of dissecting my intuitive awareness. This book is the result of study, intuitive connection, and understanding. My journey of understanding has not ended with its publication.

When I happened upon the work of Howard Gardner and Karen D. Olsen, I had an epiphany. Something clicked inside of me. Through their books, I reframed intuition not as a sixth sense, but as one sense with multiple facets through which we see and engage the world. Intuition was not a magic knowing but a means of processing information through multiple intelligences.

Mindfulness practice, neuroscience, and Emotional Intelligence provided additional pieces to my understanding puzzle. The foundation of this understanding is that we are all intuitive. The key to unlocking our intuition is in knowing who we are and engaging in a lifelong quest of discovering that knowing again and again and again.

I found myself writing and rewriting this book so many times until I said, "Enough!" Is it finished? Probably not. Each day I learn a bit more about intuition and the many ways it presents itself to me and the many ways I process it. This book is a beginning on the journey to identifying, deciphering, understanding, and responding to intuition.

This book is meant for you, the reader. Don't feel that you need to read it from front to back. Some of the chapters provide technical information and are quite heavy. Others invite you to engage your intuition. Skip around. See where your intuition calls you. This book is my understanding of intuition and how it guides me on my journey. May you find clarity with how intuition calls to you. May being intuitive be as natural as breathing for you.

Vanessa Hurst: August 2020

Chapter 1

Intuition: Mystical, Magical, Mysterious

Mystical. Magical. Mysterious. Intuition is viewed with a bit of awe and a dash of fear. Does an intuitive have the ability to peer deeply into our soul, uncovering our deepest secrets? Perhaps. Do they have a special connection to the beyond, the other? Yes, but we all have this connection.

What stops us from being intuitive? Our fear prevents us from recognizing our connection to intuition. With this book, I provide resources to strengthen your connection to inner wisdom. By creating a bridge from your logical/analytical being and your creative/intuitive one, you learn to identify, decipher, understand, and respond to your intuition.

As many masters have suggested, begin where you are. Do not be overwhelmed by identifying or processing intuition. You are already, to some degree, identifying, deciphering, understanding, and responding to your intuition. This book is an access point to deepening your understanding of how intuition speaks to you while gaining a new understanding of the role of intuition in your life.

I cannot say this enough: Everyone is intuitive. Begin with this premise. Say it over and over again until you believe it. With your belief comes a perception shift. As you gain a better intuitive understanding about how and why events unfold as they do, you recognize ongoing opportunities to meet life challenges and live with soul purpose.

We all possess, to differing degrees, intuitive awareness. Where you are at this moment is your intuitive awareness baseline. This baseline is not meant for comparison to anyone else's. It gives you an idea of where you are, in this moment, on the intuitive awareness continuum. It provides information about how you currently access and process inner wisdom. As you explore the ways you perceive and process intuition, you grow along the continuum.

The floodgate of inner wisdom does not always open when we accept that we are intuitive. In fact, once we acknowledge our intuitive nature, we may despair that we cannot easily access our intuition or decipher the messages we receive. Deepening our connection takes awareness of both our intuition and what prevents us from connecting to it. Through practice, we are better able to access our intuition.

Where do we connect to our intuition? It is received through our intuitive sense. Our intuitive sense is not an independent sixth sense. It has nineteen facets: our five primary senses and fourteen secondary senses. These are discussed in-depth in Chapters 5 and 6. Our intuitive awareness activates through one or more intuitive sense facets. When we are mindful, we are better able to hear the intuitive messages presenting through these facets.

How do we decipher our intuition? We process it with the eight intelligences identified by Howard Gardner. Emotional Intelligence, mindfulness, and neural synchrony are also vital processing components. These, too, are discussed in later chapters.

Let's dispel the fallacy that those who are more creative or engage in right-brain activities have easier access to their intuition. By developing both right- and left-brain abilities, we strengthen the corpus callosum, the bundle of nerves that connect the right and left brain hemispheres. In doing so, we increase our ability to sense our intuition. (Please note that while I have found no scientific evidence for the role of the corpus callosum in intuition, it is responsible for communication between the right and left brain hemispheres.)

Intuitive awareness grows through intentional practice and mindful awareness. With awareness, we recognize how our fears prevent us from accessing this valuable internal guidance. With intuitive courage, we recognize that that our fears need not paralyze us. The journey along the intuitive awareness continuum demands that we not ignore fears; rather, we must confront them. This confrontation is not aggressive or violent; it is the compassionate assertion that results from responding to intuitive guidance.

In confronting our fears, we gain clarity about what is stopping us from listening to our inner wisdom. Then, with courage and curious daring, we act upon our intuition despite our uncertainty. For example: Perhaps we feel the need to reach out to a friend but worry about their reaction. Acknowledging our fear, we respond to the nudge, call the friend, and discover they needed to talk. Verification of an intuitive nudge increases confidence in our ability to respond at the right time, with the right words, and with the right actions.

It is not enough to accept that we are intuitive. We must act upon our intuition. Deciphering and understanding the message provides guidance. This begins with discernment or perceiving the difference between our intuitive knowing and distractions i.e., those things that pull us out of the moment and into reaction. We dig deeply into the roots of what obscures our intuition — our fears and uncertainties. In doing so, we clear the path of intuitive response.

Cultivating a mindful stance strengthens our connection to inner knowing. Through it, we recognize the role of distractions and fears. They are not barriers; rather, they are tools we use to increase our ability to stay in the present moment and connect to intuitive messages. When we are fully engaged in the moment, we can adopt the stance of the objective observer. In this stance, we are aware of our distractions and fears but do not let them overwhelm us.

With the stance of the objective observer, we engage in full-body listening, a mindfulness practice. This requires that we enter into a state of hyperawareness in which we notice with all our senses. We listen with the four aspects of our self — our body, mind, spirit, and heart. Benedict of Nursia referred to this as listening "with the ear of the heart." Becoming adept in listening with our full being — all of our senses and the four aspects — requires practice. Full-body listening is the best means of identifying, deciphering, understanding, and responding to intuition.

Once our intuitive message is identified, we discern to understand the guidance. Reflection, introspection, and integration are integral to intuitive discernment. (See appendix for information on RI^2.) Using both reflection, an activity of the heart, and introspection, an activity of the head, we decipher intuitive messages. Reflection requires that we notice without judgment or defense. Introspection asks that we objectively decipher the message. Through integration, we actively respond to the message.

The corpus callosum, or the connector of the brain hemispheres, is vital to intuitive awareness. When the connection is strong, both sides of the brain communicate more easily with one another. The result is full brain engagement. With full brain engagement, we more readily identify internal and external intuitive stimuli. We filter distractions from intuition and respond intuitively.

Through full brain engagement, we recognize how our responses are echoes of the connection to our intuition and how our reactions are the result of being caught by our distractions. To shift from a reactionary stance to one of response, we consciously listen to our body, mind, and emotions to gain information about how we get drawn from the moment.

Full-Body Listening

Through full-body listening, a mindful practice, we identify the ways we react somatically to stimuli. For example: we may feel a tightness in our shoulders, feel short of breath, or break out into a cold sweat. We use these clues gained through full-body listening to understand the cause, distraction or intuition, of these sensations. Clarity gained, we integrate what we learn through full-body listening, and each response moves us along the intuitive awareness continuum.

How does full-body listening work? Consciously using all of our senses, we gain information about our somatic responses. Try this: Breathe into your body. Identify a sensation. Next, ask what the sensation looks like, sounds like, smells like, tastes like, and feels like. Draw a multi-sensory picture of what your body is telling you. Through this practice, you gain a holistic image of your body's monologue. This monologue includes both distractions and intuition. With practice you can separate the intuitive cues from the distractions.

Try this: the next time you meet someone, notice your physical reactions. These reactions may be positive, benign, or cautionary. Accepting that physical reactions are signs that your inner wisdom is attempting to get your attention, spend time in reflection and introspection. What are your physical reactions telling you? Then, remember a time that you ignored your intuitive warning system and engaged the other person. Recalling the memory, spend time in reflection and introspection. What did you discover about the reasons behind your physical feeling of unease or of joy?

No matter how adept we become at identifying, deciphering, understanding, and responding to our intuition, intuitive understanding is not the magical elixir that creates a perfect, angst-free life. Responding to intuition does not make all right in our world. It provides insights into our challenges, life lessons, and soul purpose. In these insights, lie opportunities for growth and transformation.

Intuitive insight provides us with another way of looking at a situation or a person. To gain clarity, we assume the stance of objective observer by being open, non-judgmental, and non-defensive. No longer judging, we are hyperaware of what we discover. We recognize opportunities and possibilities to reframe our life situation and embrace our life purpose. The personal transformation that results is the primary function of our intuitive sense.

Intuition as a Life Skill

I cannot say this enough: Intuition is not supernatural nor is it a special power only a few have. Intuition allows us to see the world with fresh eyes. Instead of seeing the finite, we perceive the infinite extraordinary. We see the world as it truly is — filled with limitless possibilities. We choose Albert Einstein's latter way of living: "There are two ways to live your life. One is as though nothing is a miracle. The other is as if everything is a miracle."

Within each miracle is a shift in our perception. Dion Fortune has said, "Magic is the art of changing consciousness at will." Through our intuitive awareness, we shift our consciousness, entering hyperawareness. In this place of seeing the extraordinary, we connect more deeply to our inner wisdom.

Through our intuition, we gain ways to heal our self and the world by connecting with our self and others on increasingly deeper, more authentic levels. In this spiral of deepening awareness, we enter the extraordinary, the home of intuitive information. The extraordinary does not have a physical location; rather, it manifests when we perceive the world through new eyes or when we change our consciousness at will.

With each change of consciousness, we experience the world as increasingly more interconnected. We dissolve the illusion of separateness. We perceive the world as a community of awakened and unawakened intuitives. We recognize that in every moment we receive information individually and collectively. For example: when I am in sync with individual or a group, we may all have the same idea or a similar one at the same time. By sharing these insights, we strengthen our connections to one another and increase the likelihood of recognizing and validating group intuition.

Although we live in community, intuition is birthed in our authentic self. Through our authentic self we access our intuitive sense facets and create pathways through which we process intuitive messages. Starting at our intuitive awareness baseline, we identify the more accessible ways we gain information. This assessment is vital to our intuitive journey.

Start Where You Are

Spiritual masters recommend that we "start where we are." This is great advice for our journey with intuition. There is no wrong place to begin; no level of acceptance of or experience with intuition is too little. Each response to intuitive knowing nudges us along our personal intuitive awareness continuum. Although it may be difficult not to judge or compare our intuitive self to another, it is through the stance of the objective observer that we let go of our need to judge or compare. With objectivity, we identify, decipher, and respond to our inner wisdom.

We start where are. Our intent is not to become more intuitive, but to increase our response to our intuition. Strengthening intuitive awareness and increasing our intuitive response is fourfold. First, we accept we are intuitive. Even if we are unable to recognize our nudges as intuition, we affirm that we are intuitive. Second, we affirm our abilities each time we recognize a nudge. Third, we actively decipher any intuitive message. Fourth, we respond using the information received.

Seldom does anyone have the ability to identify, decipher, understand, and respond to inner wisdom 100 percent of the time. Even when we accept that we are intuitive, we still miss a number of intuitive cues. This is due, in part, to our conditioning to ignore our intuition, and as a result, sabotage our connection to inner knowing.

Although we have been connected to our intuition since birth, we have diminished access to this connection due to life events. We may also have a suspicion of things that are not rational or cannot be proven. These are not insurmountable challenges. We overcome our challenges through a paradigm shift. Connecting to our intuition requires a childlike wonder and awe in which we see the extraordinary in the world.

We practice. We verify. We gain confidence in our abilities. Through the spiral of intuitive awareness, we forge new, stronger connections with our intuition. It is inevitable that no matter how skilled we are, we will miss some intuitive messages. We need not fear that we are missing something important. Any important intuitive cue returns again and again and again until we can no longer ignore it. That is a constant we can trust.

As with our abilities, how we define the source of our information is different for each of us. No matter what we name as the source, our intuition is a life guide. Intuition is the power that impels us along our life path. With its guidance, we meet challenges, learn life lessons, and live our soul purposes. Intuitive messages are kernels of knowledge that, when acknowledged and integrated into our lives, bring growth and transformation.

Accepting that we are intuitive is the single, most important step to take in living our soul purpose. Through our perception shifts, we practice connecting to the information received in our heart — intuition — with our head — understanding. We discover our current intuitive limits and push out our boundaries in ways that move us along the intuitive awareness continuum.

When our intuition is befriended, we create the sacred space necessary for this connection to flourish. This sacred space is both internal and external. Within this environment, we not only access inner wisdom but also learn to trust it unconditionally. Internal knowing fuels external response and ricochets back into our self to strengthen the pathway for intuitive understanding. We notice the intuitive cues in greater frequency. Our sacred mosaic expands into the whole of our life.

In moments of hyperawareness, we become receptive to embracing our intuitive nature. We accept that we are intuitive beings. We access the limitless source of inspiration, growth, and transformation that is our intuition. Connecting the mosaic's tiles intuitively, we are nudged into the rhythm of our life purpose.

Mystical? Yes. Mysterious? Yes. Magical? Yes. Inaccessible? No. Each of us is intuitive. Through practice and experience, we befriend our inner wisdom. Consciously and unconsciously, we respond to our intuition. Moving into an intimate relationship with intuition, we realize a world that is no longer only mundane; we intuitively wake and are aware of the extraordinary. Through this connection we evolve as individuals and as a collective.

Chapter 2

Into the Extraordinary

We inhabit three realities at the same time — the extraordinary, the mundane, and the between. As stated earlier, each reality has a specific role in accessing, interpreting, understanding, and responding to our intuition.

• The mundane is the world in which we live. It is also the place in which we respond to our intuitive messages.

• The extraordinary is the access point of our intuition. As our perception shifts, we enter the extraordinary through hyperawareness. Through this paradigm shift, the extraordinary and mundane integrate. Our interactions in the mundane reflect this integration.

• The between is a bridge on which we decipher information. We process our intuitive messages from the extraordinary and fashion a response. Leaving the bridge, we come full circle as we respond intuitively in the mundane.

We live in the mundane world. At times we are aware; other times, we live on autopilot. By awakening to our intuition, our perception shifts. By increasing our awareness in the moment, we shift from the mundane. We notice the extraordinary in the world. With this shift, we see and hear the many ways our intuition speaks. Unless our attention is focused in the moment, we return to autopilot and disconnect from our intuition.

No matter how mindful we are, it is inevitable that we lose focus. We are pulled back into the mundane by distractions. For the purpose of this book, a distraction is something that prevents us from connect-ing to our inner wisdom. "Distracted" need not be a permanent condition. When we notice how distractions hook us, we refocus our attention and return to the extraordinary world of intuitive awareness.

Intuition requires that we travel the triad realms of the mundane, the extraordinary, and the between — the bridge connecting the mundane and extraordinary. All three worlds are equally important. We do not want to segregate ourselves from the mundane. This realm is our everyday life. Here our interactions are both aware and unaware. The extraordinary is the place of engaged hyperawareness and connection with our intuition. In the between, we decipher the messages found in the extraordinary. We act upon what we decipher in the mundane.

As we move throughout the triad realities, we notice both our intuition and the many ways we get distracted. As we move along the intuitive awareness continuum, we become more skilled in separating distractions from our inner knowing. Distractions are not bad. Part of intuitive awareness is being aware of how we get distracted.

Thomas Merton was aware that, "In modern life our senses are so constantly bombarded with stimulation from every side that unless we develop a kind of protective insensibility we would go crazy trying to respond." The twenty-first century has seen an explosion of information. At any given moment, we can access information about most any subject. The internet, 24-hour news channels, and e-books are immediately available. We need to find a way to identify distractions and protect our self from them.

Unless we can learn to listen to both internal and external stimuli, we will suffer from information fatigue. While some of the bombardment improves our life and encourages development of our quiet mind, many distractions prevent us from being truly present. Some distractions push us into the past where we ruminate on regrets, guilt, and grief. Others propel us into the future filling us with hopes and dreams, worries and fears. Distractions cloud our mind and create barriers of illusion. Without a mindfulness practice, we are unable to separate our intuition from distractions.

Silence

Within a cultivated environment of silence, we gain clarity. It becomes easier to filter the distractions from inner wisdom. With our minds clear, we recognize the voice of our intuition speaking through our intuitive sense facets. Listening to this voice, we are better able to identify and decipher our intuition. This listening brings understanding and response.

The line between intuition and distraction is thin. At times, we may be sure that our intuition is speaking only to determine later that we were distracted. Intuition and distraction present differently. Our inner wisdom invites us to be mindful of what is unfolding. A distraction triggers a reaction that pulls us away from the moment. Once we recognize how the signs of distraction impact us, we get better at recognizing when our intuition speaks and separating distractions from intuitive messages.

Only within silence can we discern the difference between a distraction and our intuition. What is silence? It is easier to begin with what silence is not. It is not a vacuum of nothingness. It is not a lack of noise. Silence is a place of clarity. It is the foundation of our ability to be present in the moment. When in the environment of silence, we are alert to what is unfolding and choose to respond authentically.

Silence manifests in our minds, hearts, and spirits. It is reflected in our fourth aspect, the body. Our physical sensations tell us if we are peaceful and calm or distracted and harried. The silence that cultivates mindfulness is foundational to clarity gained through full-body listening. In an environment of silence, we listen with all of our senses and note the world's impact on us. When we are hyperaware, the world presents differently.

Full-body listening can only be accomplished in an environment of silence. Through it, we gather information from our intuitive sense facets as it manifests in our four aspects — body, mind, spirit, and heart. Our intuition manifests as physical sensations in our body, our thoughts or verbal and visual patterns in our mind, felt emotions, or a connection to something greater than us. Intuition is truly a full-body, multi-sensory experience.

In order to access our intuition, we foster an inner peace that is foundational to objectivity. As an objective observer, we discern by using full-body listening. (See the Appendix for more on full-body listening.) This includes attending to voice cadence and body language. Even the awareness of pheromones, what attracts us to another, provides clues. We engage our intuitive sense facets to sift through the information, discount any distractions, and identify the message. We gain clarity as we note what prevents us from hearing the intuitive resonance in the four aspects.

When we are mindful, we are alert to our intuition. For example: We feel a cold shiver running down our spine. We hear a word or phrase or see an image in our mind's eye. We feel emotions and recognize that they are not ours. These sensations signal us to pay attention, to notice how intuition speaks to us through our four aspects.

Distractions

Within silence, our attention is focused, our senses primed. We are better able to differentiate distractions from intuition. Remember, anything that pulls us from the moment is a distraction. Distractions are not always negative; at times they fill us with joy and happiness. Although we react positively, these distractions still pull us from the moment. By identifying distractions, we gain the ability to neutralize their effects.

All is not lost when we are caught by a distraction. Even when we are hooked, we have the ability to name the distraction and release it. No longer distracted, we can objectively focus on the extraordinary. As an objective observer, we are a hyperaware "engager" who notices how we get tripped by our distractions. For example: instead of the words of another becoming triggers, we hear the words, feel the rise of our emotions, and choose to not get caught in reaction. Intuitively aware, we are not compromised by a distraction. Think of distractions as permeable barriers we pass through to hear our intuition.

Getting caught in distractions or shenpa lessens the more aware we become. (Shenpa is a Buddhist term for what prevents us from being fully present.) When caught in shenpa, we attach to feelings, people, or things in order to feel better. Shenpa is a permeable barrier that prevents us from hearing our intuition. Distracted, we convince our self that everything is all right; we cannot sense our intuition. We are unable to respond in ways that bring transformation.

A distraction is benign until it catches us in a loop of being pulled from the moment, followed by reacting, followed by being pulled farther from the moment. Caught in shenpa, we disconnect from our inner wisdom. The way to reconnection is through clarity that results from cultivated silence. We identify what catches us and avoid the trap of distraction. With shenpa unhooked, inner wisdom becomes a stronger life navigator.

Another benefit of listening and responding to our intuition is increased neuroplasticity of our brain. If our brain is "plastic," we are more flexible and responsive. We more easily identify our intuition, decipher it, and choose how to respond. Flexible and open to new ways of being, we create new patterns of response. The result is synaptic pruning, a wiring of new patterns in the brain. This rewiring provides a strengthened connection to our intuition.

As our brain increases in plasticity, we are more adept in recognizing the difference between distractions and intuition. Distractions become more visible; we re-pattern reactions into responses. With this reframing, we gain greater clarity. This clarity increases the stability of silence in our quiet mind. Our trust in our ability to recognize and respond to the whispers of wisdom increases. We become more receptive to our intuition.

Into the Extraordinary

No matter where we are on the intuitive awareness continuum, silence must be continually nurtured and deepened. This occurs through mindful practice. Some mindfulness activities are meditation, journaling, art creation, and physical exercise. I believe that any activity through which we gain clarity is a mindful one. Cultivated mindfulness is key to entering the extraordinary, home of our intuitive messages.

Our intuitive awareness flourishes within the extraordinary. If you are unclear about how the extraordinary is present in your life, spend time reflecting upon what you hold in reverence. Identify where and how this deep respect informs your life. Please note that your relationship with the extraordinary is not static. What you viewed as extraordinary four years ago may be very different than today. Months or even moments from now your extraordinary may shift again. Accepting its dynamic and evolving properties moves you along your intuitive awareness continuum.

For example: for me, the extraordinary is a shift in my awareness. I may notice the beauty in a bird's flight, a truth in a person's words, or the intuitive nature of a dream. The extraordinary manifests for me as I breathe into the moment and vow to take nothing at face value. When I adopt a stance of wide openness, intuition manifests in the most surprising ways.

Strengthening our connection to the extraordinary is imperative to increasing our connection to intuition. I have found that within the extraordinary my recognition of distractions increases while the noise of distractions diminishes. We hear beyond the distractions to identify intuition. The pathway through the mundane, extraordinary, and between is the path of neuroplasticity. Through synaptic pruning we create new pathways to decipher, understand, and respond to our intuition.

My conscious journey to living in the extraordinary began with formal contemplative practice. I committed to periods of meditation. Within this silence, I sifted through distractions and inner wisdom. As my intuitive clarity increased, I trusted what I was receiving. My confidence increased.

Fostering Mindfulness

Increased mindfulness enhances our intuitive abilities. We deepen intuitive awareness through a personalized routine of contemplative practice. There is no one size fits all when developing a contemplative routine or becoming more intuitively aware. We experiment until we find a practice that resonates with our inner wisdom.

Not all meditative activities foster mindfulness for all of us. Some may find certain practices distractive. For example: I am easily distracted during twenty minutes or more of sitting meditation. By identifying this, I choose more appropriate practices to increase my intuitive awareness. These meditative practices include walking the labyrinth and journaling.

Meditation is a way of engaging our intuition. Through this focused attention, we form a bridge from our intent to our action. This bridge provides focus and brings clarity. It connects our internal wisdom with our external actions. The bridge is the framework through which we intuitively experience the present moment.

Our intuitive awareness thrives when we regularly engage in a three-fold way of intuitive engagement: meditation, focused intent, and contemplation. Meditation refines our awareness and creates a bridge to intuitive awareness. Meditation and focused intent strengthen our connection to inner wisdom. During the third element, contemplation, we actively listen to the voice of intuition. We full-body listen with our intuitive sense facets. With contemplation, we tap into the extraordinary to identify our intuition.

The more we practice this three-fold way of intuitive engagement, the easier it is to spontaneously move into clarity. To span the gap from inner wisdom to conscious knowing, we actively cultivate silence. Through silence we access our quiet mind, the repository of intuition.

Within our quiet mind, we create our personal view of reality, which includes both truth and illusion. Our quiet mind is like a tree. Our thoughts are the woody parts of the tree. Our words and actions are the leaves and flowers. At the root of our quiet mind are our judgments, beliefs, and assumptions. We can only grow a strong tree by listening and responding to our intuition while negating the judgments and assumptions that give birth to our distractions.

Our intuitive awareness nourishes all aspects of our quiet mind. Through it, we connect our rational thoughts with our emotional, creative center. This connection increases our ability to recognize our intuition and decipher it. Our corpus callosum is strengthened through this connection. Our right and left brain hemispheres communicate more fully. Without this strong right and left brain connection, our mindfulness is diminished; we are lost in the buzz of distraction.

Within the white noise of distraction, we get caught. The tangles of distraction obliterate the whispers of intuition. We react. This does not have to be an endless loop of distraction and reaction. We can return to the moment by focusing our attention, reforming our intent, and quietly listening. Through meditation, we identify the barriers to our intuition. In contemplation, we listen to our inner wisdom and gain ways to dismantle barriers.

The process of meditation, statement of intent, and contemplation occurs in our quiet mind. It is the powerhouse of clarity. We dig into our quiet mind to discover what is preventing a deeper connection to our inner wisdom. As we remove the roots that grow our distractions, our connection to intuition grows. This is synaptic pruning. As we re-pattern, we identify the illusions, give voice to our truth, and own our intuition as a powerful guide to transforming to our true self.

Silence, quiet mind, and intuition are all necessary to unlocking the door that separates the mundane and the extraordinary. One is not more important than another. Each operates separately. Silence is the environment; the quiet mind brings clarity and awareness; intuition is the message. All three are necessary to identify, decipher, understand, and respond to our intuition.

Even if our quiet mind is free of illusions, without silence, our ability to clearly sense the intuitive message is diminished. When the quiet mind rests in silence, awareness is raised. We hear the voice of intuition. We begin to navigate our life challenges and live our soul purpose as we separate distractions from intuitive nudges.

Try this: Recall a conversation that unsettled you. Listen to what your internal monologue says. Use your primary senses to describe the conversation. What was your intuition saying to you? Did you listen to what your intuition relayed? Why or why not?

When we listen to our intuition, we gain a greater understanding of what is stopping us from living our soul purpose. (Soul purpose is the reason for our being.) Living our soul purpose, we connect with our true self; our intuitive being flourishes. We gather information without question or judgment. We see the microcosm and the macrocosm — we see not only the message but how it connects to the whole of our life. This way of perceiving empowers us intuitively.

Awareness leads us past the temptation of arguing and mistrust. Each time we avoid disbelief, it becomes easier to trust our inner wisdom. Do we practice trusting our intuition until we wake up one morning totally connected to it? Once connected, do we ever have to worry about being disconnected from our intuition? The answer to both these questions is no. While we are never 100 percent aware of our intuition, we are never totally disconnected from it. Whether we recognize its guiding force or not, intuition is with us always. Even when we are unaware, we respond intuitively.

Intuitive Awareness and Growth Mindset

Intuitive awareness requires a growth mindset. Carol Dweck in Mindset: The New Psychology of Success states that we approach the world in two ways: with a fixed mindset or with a growth mindset. Few of us approach the world totally in one or the other. When we have a fixed mindset, we do things without questioning and seldom explore outside our comfort zone. We have difficulty with change. When we assume a growth mindset, we thrive in dynamic, fluid environments. We are naturally curious, daring, and courageous.

Although someone with a growth mindset finds avenues to intuition more easily accessible, unless they continue the practice of meditation, statement of intent, and contemplation, their connection to inner wisdom and their intuitive awareness becomes static. With a growth mindset, even if the tumult increases, the ability to discern inner wisdom is not diminished.

Accessing our intuition is a never-ending cycle of nurturing the environment of silence, resting in our quiet mind, and being mindfully aware. With a growth mindset, we act in ways that increase our intuitive awareness. We live as a change agent who powers personal transformation through inner wisdom. We understand that practice is every-thing. Practice forms our experience. Through experience, we identify intuitive knowing, understand the messages, and formulate responses.

Through silence and the quiet mind, we clear debris from the path-way of intuition. This pathway opens to us through our nineteen intu-itive sense facets. Intuitive awareness unlocks each facet. Peering deeply into the extraordinary, we gather information from our sense facets us-ing full-body listening. We discover that while some facets are more eas-ily accessible, with practice, we access information from all of them.

Awareness is everything. When we are in the moment, we notice how our intuition is speaking to us and how our distractions get in the way of intuition's voice. Being intuitively aware asks that we are awake to each moment, alert to both intuitive messages and distractions, and alive to the realization that we have the capacity to live an intuitively re-sponsive life. Through a3 awareness we become change agents who rely upon our intuition in every moment of every day.

Chapter 3

a3 awareness: awake, alert, alive

When we are open to experiencing inexplicable knowing, we enter that mysterious, magical, mystical place of intuition and gain information about living our soul purpose. This hyperaware state is being fully awake, fully alert, fully alive. We inhabit three realities at the same time — the extraordinary, the mundane, and the between. In the mundane, we respond to our intuitive messages. The extraordinary is the access point of our intuition. The between is a bridge on which we decipher information. Leaving the bridge, we come full circle as we respond intuitively in the mundane.

a3 awareness

Moving consciously through the mundane, the extraordinary, and the between is possible when we are awake, alert, and alive — the essence of a3 awareness. When we are awake, we are less like likely to lose moments of time. Reflect on this: how often have you driven from Point A to Point B only to realize that you were not mentally awake to the actual trip? When awake, we notice how the extraordinary twines with the mundane. Our ability to notice what is extraordinary is heightened. For example: we may hear the words of another and identify the intuitive message within.

Being alert is maintaining a state of curious vigilance. We are prepared to formulate a response to information identified during our awake moments. Being alive is the result of being awake and alert. In these moments we fearlessly decipher the message of our intuition and prepare a courageous response. Alive we seamlessly integrate our intuitive knowing into our responses. As an intuitive who engages in a3 awareness, we are a confident walker amid worlds — the mundane, the extraordinary, and the between.

Our intuitive GPS activates in the extraordinary. Our senses notice what does not resonate authentically to us. We also gain clues to how distractions impact us. The more familiar we become with how intuition speaks, the greater our ability to separate distraction from truth. Even if we are not able to put into words what seems wrong, our intuition alerts us through sensations in one of our four aspects. Through reflection and introspection, we name the message of our intuition.

Unless we are alert, we are unable to formulate a response to our intuition. Although being awake anchors us into the moment, it is with curious vigilance that we catch any nuggets of wisdom. Being awake and vigilantly alert to the messages of intuition empowers us to identify, decipher, and understand our intuition. Through the third "a" — alive — we respond to our intuition.

Some may argue that the fact that we breathe means we are alive. And, we are. But when we engage each moment mindfully, our perception shifts. We see the extraordinary hidden in plain sight. We choose to respond from that reality. When we are alive in this way, we consciously incorporate our intuition into each thought, word, and action.

Once a3 awareness is our primary way of being in the world, our perspective permanently shifts. We sense intuitive messages in the words of another, in something being out of order, in a whisper in our internal monologue — the ways to sense our intuition are endless. Accurately deciphering these cues is foundational to positive interactions with the world. We gain clarity as to why we chose what we chose. Being aware gives meaning to our choices.

A3 awareness requires bare attention or focusing attention objectively, without an agenda. With bare attention, we practice the 4nons — non-attachment, non-judgment, non-defensiveness, and nonviolence to gain greater understanding. (See the Appendix for more information on the 4nons.) We identify the many ways we label and judge, but we choose not to use labels or judgments as foundations for reaction.

Through the practice of bare attention, the differences between distractions and intuition are more easily discernible. Potential meanings surface. Engaged in full-body listening, we decipher intuitive messages. Even if we cannot understand the entirety of the message, we may be able to understand bits of it. With bare attention, we navigate the mundane, the extraordinary, and the between to use the whole or pieces of an intuitive cue to identify, decipher, and understand our intuition in order to create our responses.

Intuition and the Triad Realities

We live in three intertwined worlds — the mundane, the between, and the extraordinary. An intuitive consciously and intentionally walks amid these worlds. Even if we live in the mundane for the majority of the time, we all have moments of accessing the extraordinary. As we move along the intuitive awareness continuum, we are less likely to get stuck in the mundane by distractions. Increasingly, we live in all three worlds simultaneously.

When we believe "why not," we are fully present to the extraordinary. Colors may seem brighter, joy sharper, love sweeter. What we see is not equal to the sum of all parts; rather, it appears greater, deeper, more vibrant as we access our intuitive awareness. Within this place of limitless possibilities our intuition thrives. We gather intuitive material. We use this material to fashion a response in the between.

The between is a place of limitless potential, curiosity, and daring. Within the between we feed our potential and open to possibilities. We decipher intuitive information and form responses. Any activity in the between is only possible through an atmosphere of silence. Without the clarity gained in silence, distractions overwhelm us and our ability to interpret intuition is limited.

We've learned about the three realms, but how do we navigate them? Without awareness, entering the extraordinary may catch us by surprise. Through a word, an action, or an image we may find our self in the extraordinary. For example: as I sat in a coffee shop discerning if I would apply for a job, a woman struck up a conversation with me. Her intuition led her to engage me. I was surprised to learn that she had previously held the position I was considering applying for. Our conversation validated my intuitive concerns about the position, but I still applied.

During a second interview for the job, the voices of my intuition that had urged caution began to make sense. I was not compatible with the job nor was the job compatible to me. After having that realization, my body became noticeably lighter; the world seemed filled with potential. I connected to all three realms simultaneously as I understood what my intuition had been relaying.

One might ask if I should have listened to the whispers earlier in the process and not applied for the position. I believe that I needed to apply. Circumstances in the mundane required an application submission. Holding the awareness of my concerns allowed me to not take what happened personally during the interview. I connected with some great people, one of whom helped me refashion my résumé and refine my job search.

Moving between the three realms and integrating the wisdom of intuition into our life journey is not a science. It requires that we refine our listening skills, trust any inner knowing we receive, and be confident in our ability to decipher it. Our intuitive awareness is fluid and evolving. When we understand this; our confidence grows, and we learn new ways of deciphering.

This might mean using skills from both hemispheres of our brain and strengthening our corpus callosum. We engage the left side for logic, analysis, and research skills. We engage the right for creativity. We free associate using both sides of our brain. When we are fluid in engaging our intuition, deciphering becomes dynamic. Intuitive awareness becomes a true guide for life navigation. Engaging life in these three realities empowers us to listen with our intuitive sense and respond with our heart. We walk amid these worlds with increasing surety and confidence.

Chapter 4

Being a Change Agent

Being intuitive means embracing our inner change agent. When we open to the potential of change no matter how scary or uncomfortable, we more easily identify those nudges of intuition. As we decipher, we look beyond the surface interpretation to find subtle nuances in the intuitive message. Not everyone is a natural change agent. Shifting our paradigm to being a receptive change agent requires patience. As a change agent, we become increasingly more adept in both understanding and integrating our inner wisdom into our interactions. With practice and commitment, we move along the intuitive awareness continuum.

At birth, we are fully connected, fully aware of our innate wisdom. From our first breath, we are intuitively aware, but we lack the ability to communicate our inner wisdom in this new world. As we learn to communicate and experience the traumas of integration, the connection to our intuition is frayed. Our ability to access our intuition lessens. Although we may have forgotten how to consciously access and process our intuition, we never lose the ability.

As we learn to communicate with the world, a breach forms between our intuition and our consciousness that prevents us from knowingly interacting with the mundane, between, and extraordinary. We can re-learn to consciously traverse the triad realities. To rebuild our connection, we attend to our senses in different ways. Through listening, experiencing, and practicing, we repair our ability to access intuition. A bridge forms across the breach.

Remember, no special skills or education is required to connect to our intuition. All that is required is a shift in our awareness. The practice of a3 awareness or being awake, alert, and alive opens access to the bridge. Through this access we gain clarity of our intuitive voice and receive the power to act upon it. With intuitive clarity, we recreate a way of seeing the world.

This intuitive way of being is experienced through the triad realities. As our navigation skills improve, we no longer engage in three separate realities; they seamlessly become one.

Each time we access our intuition, we are given the ability to perceive people and circumstances differently. This altered perception opens our mind and nudges us out of complacency. Our world becomes one of latent potential waiting to be activated. We live within possibility. What was once viewed as insurmountable is reframed as opportunity for growth. We learn from our challenges. Intuition is a chief transformer.

Intuition seeds the power of transformation. It provides cues that are deciphered and discerned through reflection and introspection. For example: I might question a difficulty that I am having with a friend. I reflect upon the issue setting my intent to be open to whatever I need to understand. The answer comes in the form of intuitive cues.

As an objective observer, I better hear the voices that waft from my intuition. By recognizing these intuitive cues, I have a better chance of accurately deciphering the message. No matter if these messages are simple or complex, I am nudged to respond. I may call a friend, read a book, discern a new job, make a decision about a relationship. By listening to inner wisdom, we access guidance in every aspect of our being.

Although we may be aware or unaware of the intuitive messages we receive, a change agent perceives the fluid, dynamic nature of life. We are not afraid of triggers. For us, triggers are opportunities to use our intuition to neutralize a reaction while fashioning a response. A change agent moves fluidly amid the extraordinary, mundane, and between as we actively search for meaning and purpose.

Walking amid the three worlds, a change agent listens to how the voice of intuition is bringing attention to potential reactions and responses. Our mantra is to know our authentic self in an effort to discern intuitive knowings. Distractions are not seen as foes; they are wisdom teachers. By focusing on the potential of an intuitive message, a change agent actively seeks insights and uses bare attention to decipher the cues in the between.

On this wild ride between realities, it is easy to get carried away by our intuitive abilities. A humble heart is a prerequisite of bare attention. While acknowledging our intuitive skills, we realize that we do not know all the answers; we do not always decipher our intuition correctly. With humility, we seek to connect to our intuition in ways that draw us closer to our soul purpose.

We are not better than another because we are conscious of our intuition. In fact, intuitive awareness makes us more aware of when we miss information. As an intuitive, we are grateful when we meet our life challenges, learn our lessons, and live our soul purpose. Through our intuitive awareness we live from our authentic core.

Intuition and Critical Thinking

With a3 awareness, we gain the resources necessary for critical thinking. Through it, we objectively evaluate assumptions and recognize the potential impact of judgments and assumptions that are left unchecked. We recognize how they are the foundation of distractions and misinterpreted intuition.

As our barriers are dismantled, we respond in nonreactive, less defensive, non-judgmental ways. This stance is the base of being an objective observer. A change agent practices bare attention as we remove our nonfunctioning filters they have been damaged by judgments and assumptions. We perceive what is actually happening. Our triggers and potential reactions are illuminated. We navigate the minefield of distraction with the guidance of intuition.

With bare attention, we are no longer blinded by our fears. While our instinct may be to react with fear, bare attention guides us in the acknowledgement and befriending of our fears. Only when our fears are no longer enemies can we craft a peaceful response. Using the 4nons assures that instead of twisting the information to meet our wants, we decipher the information without attachment, judgment, defensiveness, or violence. We critically engage our intuition. We respond with honesty.

Being a change agent is more than being receptive to transformation. With this mindset we open to seeing the world differently and living in true reflection of our soul purpose. We willingly ask questions and full-body listen to the answers. We power our lives by reframing and seeking the best ways to live our potential. This happens by listening with our intuitive sense and responding to the world with our intuition.

Chapter 5

Our Intuitive Sense, The Primary Facets

Our intuitive sense is not a sixth sense. It is comprised of at least nineteen sense facets that are described in this book. Receptive to seeing beyond the mundane world, we actively engage these senses to discover meaning. As we gather information from different sense facets, we notice how our intuitive messages vie for our attention. Some whispers are louder and more easily heard while others are barely recognizable and easily missed. By focusing on the facets with louder intuitive voices, we become more trusting of our skills and more capable of identifying more of our intuitive cues.

In time, we gain the confidence to explore the intuitive sense facets or the speakers of wisdom's whispers. These facets are not found in a nebulous sixth sense. Our intuition is heard, seen, felt, sensed within a full-body experience of listening with all nineteen intuitive sense facets. As with everything, we begin where we are. We connect to our intuitive awareness through the primary facets, our five senses: sight, hearing, taste, smell, and touch.

Instead of identifying one single intuitive sense, let's think in terms of nineteen facets within one intuitive sense. The first five senses are our primary senses. The other fourteen are what I call secondary sense facets. These deeper ways of accessing our intuition activate through a3 aware-ness or being fully awake, fully alert, and fully alive. Through this en-gaged awareness we intuitively listen and respond.

Our intuitive sense facets provide a gateway into the extraordinary. Karen D. Olsen has identified the nineteen senses that I refer to as our intuitive sense facets. Knowledge of these additional senses opens us to greater awareness as to how we receive information. For example: if we know we can see light beyond the visible spectrum, seeing infrared light no longer means there is something wrong with us; it means we are sensing something intuitively.

These intuitive sense facets connect our three realities: the mundane, the between, and the extraordinary. With practice, we become increasingly more proficient in using information gained through our intuitive sense facets to move between these worlds. As with all things intuitive, we start where we are with those facets we more easily access. With further practice, we gain additional information from other facets.

Discovering which facets are more easily accessible is much like discovering where we initially present on the intuitive awareness continuum. Remember, each of us accesses our intuitive sense in ways that are uniquely ours. To begin, notice which senses most often present intuitive cues. There is no wrong answer to this. Instead of getting discouraged, remind yourself that you must start somewhere. And, that somewhere is the starting point of an ever-expanding connection with intuitive awareness.

All nineteen facets are examined in this book. The first five are discussed in this chapter. The other fourteen are discussed in the next chapter. I recommend experimenting with the primary senses first. As you explore, you will notice how the other fourteen are speaking intuitively. If you are called to explore with some of the other fourteen, do so. There is no wrong way to deepen your connection to intuition. There is only your way.

Remember, this is your journey. Start, and continue, where you are guided. For me, becoming familiar with the primary sense facets led to an easier recognition of cues manifesting through the other fourteen facets. You may find yourself exploring in a different fashion.

The five primary facets are: sight, hearing, touch, taste, and smell. Each of us uses at least one of these facets to connect to our inner wisdom. To discover which ones are more easily accessed, we focus on a sense and notice how our intuition speaks through it.

RI^2 : & the Five Primary Sense Facets

If you are unclear how your intuition speaks to you, spend time in reflection and introspection noting which facets have the loudest intuitive voices. As you trust and gain confidence in your abilities to access your intuition, you become more aware of how the other facets speak to you. Let's learn more about using reflection and introspection in your journey with intuition.

- Reflection is information gathering. Begin resting in silence. Key into a specific intuitive sense facet and notice. For example: you notice what you see with your eyes open and closed. Eyes open, you look at the physical world. Notice what you notice. Now close your eyes, and pay attention to what you are seeing with your mind's eye. Note what information you gather.

- Introspection is deciphering not only the message, but also how it is received. We ask questions and look for patterns. We use our logic to decipher and understand the intuitive message. We create a framework of response. Write down the information you received, and then use your logical mind to listen to your intuition.

- Integration, the final step in RI^2, is responding to our intuitive messages. This is also the final step in identifying, deciphering, understanding and responding (integration) to our intuition.

Reflection and introspection occur in the between. The third part of this process, the integration of what we have learned, happens in the mundane. RI^2 — reflection, introspection, and integration — is clarity building and response formulating. Reflection is a heart-centered gathering of information. Introspection is deciphering the message from our head. Integration is the active response to intuition.

Through reflection and introspection, we understand not only the mechanics of intuitive awareness, but also the message. Some messages are easily deciphered and understood while others take deeper introspection including research or being open to additional cues and reflection time. Please note: the three steps may happen in a matter of seconds or may take hours or even days. We may need to return to RI^2 several times to gain information that brings clarity.

The RI^2 process is instrumental in recognizing how we receive intuition. Use RI^2 as a means to identify, decipher, understand, and respond to information you receive from the five primary senses.

The Five Primary Sense Facets

Let's dig a little deeper into the five primary sense facets: sight, hearing, touch, taste, and smell.

Sight: For most of us, sight is the predominant sense. Our eyes may be drawn to an object, person, the written word, an animal, or some other sight. We may not even notice what we are seeing. With hyperawareness, we allow our eyes to be drawn to what we need to see intuitively. We take in information without labeling, judging, or attempting to decipher.

Seeing does not occur in a vacuum; we notice what information we receive from our other senses. This information enhances what we receive with our eyes. Seldom do we receive an intuitive nudge from one sense independent of the other senses. When I notice something with my eyes, I full-body listen using other facets to gain a more comprehensive understanding of my intuition.

Hearing: We hear noises, but, at times, the sounds do not register on a conscious level. We may be distracted by the noise but are unaware of what disturbs us. For example: I have lived both near an airport and train tracks. Over time, I experienced hearing fatigue. I no longer heard background noises and needed to depend upon other senses to alert me to sounds.

If we are not in the moment, we miss opportunities to notice and understand what we hear. We miss the message in lyrics that play on a loop in our mind. We miss the importance of a topic that surfaces again and again in conversation or on the news. When we are hyperaware, we hear underlying messages in conversations, the natural world, in lyrics, and other sounds. For example: a singing bird draws our attention, and we hear the message in its song.

Touch: Using our tactile sense facet, we feel heat and cool, roughness and smoothness, calm and frenetic. Close your eyes and sense with your physical body. This brings you to a different level of awareness. Place your hands directly on an animate or inanimate object. Describe what you are feeling without your sight interfering.

Through our sense of touch, we listen with the eyes of our hands and see with the ears of our body; we become aware of memories hidden in our physical body. We don't have to step in mud to remember what it feels like, nor do we need to plunge our hands into ice water to feel the shiver-shock. We hold somatic memories of previous experiences; our intuition unlocks them.

Taste: Conscious eating helps us to identify flavors, both subtle and pronounced. When eating, slowly chew food with your eyes closed. In doing so, you are better able to discern why you like certain foods and why others are unpalatable.

You may be unconscious of actual taste sensations when you react to intuitive nudges. You might say, "That leaves a bad taste in my mouth." When this happens, check the sensations in your mouth. How do they reflect your words? As you practice being intuitively aware with this sense, realize that this — and our sense of smell — are the least acknowledged of the primary senses.

Not all intuitive tastes are negative. "Sweet as honey" describes a joyous occasion. Try this: to become more adept in accessing information via the taste buds, mindfully describe what you are eating. Next, ask yourself what certain situations taste like. The more you practice identifying cues from lesser known primary facets like taste, the more likely you are to notice intuitive cues that come to you through two or more senses.

Smell: Our sense of smell is intricately connected with our sense of taste. Physically, we cannot have one without the other. Reflect upon what happens to your sense of taste when you are congested. Both senses are dulled. A sensation from one may encourage us into further exploration using the other.

Phantom smells are accessed with this sense. For example: I would smell nag champa incense and cinnamon. The nag champa alerts me to the presence of a guide. Cinnamon reminds me of my father who is deceased. Although the substances that triggered those aromas were not physically present, the aroma was the catalyst for me to enter into a quiet place as I listened to the voice of intuition. To begin reflection, we ask: What message did my guide wish to convey? What was the message in the memory of my father?

Creating a Multi-Sensory Intuitive Message

Although we may hear the voice of our intuition from one primary facet, the information seldom comes from only one. As we become more proficient in listening with our senses, we notice how sensations from several senses twine together to create a multi-sensory intuitive message.

Using these five facets requires mindful awareness. If we are distracted, we risk missing everything except the brightest, noisiest, most pungent, sharpest, most temperature variant intuitive nudges. With a stance of mindfulness, we maintain full-body listening. With practice we identify progressively subtle intuitive cues.

The potential for us to recognize and respond to our intuition is present in every moment. When we are aware, even the slightest whisper of intuition is amplified. It is through increased awareness of information received by our primary sense facets that our ability to traverse the mundane, the extraordinary, and the between is refined.

It is not enough that we notice the intuitive cues. Connecting our heart — reflection — to our head — introspection — creates a pathway of intuitive discernment. Being increasingly more adept intuitively requires awareness, practice, and experience. We become an adept when we not only trust that our intuition speaks to us but also have confidence that it will speak to us whenever and however we need.

Becoming adept in identifying intuitive cues and deciphering their meanings is a lifelong practice requiring courage, vulnerability, and humility. It takes courage to respond to information we have no way of validating; vulnerability to be open to mistaking a distraction from an intuitive message; and humility to accept that our consciousness is not in charge.

Our inability to be intuitively aware 100 percent of the time is not a failure. By reflecting upon where, when, and how we missed an intuitive nudge, we gain insights about where we should focus our attention. Being intuitively aware is living in complete trust and faith that we are our own guide. When we accept that we are intuitive, we commit to a lifelong journey of moving along the intuitive awareness continuum.

The use of RI^2 to identify, decipher, understand, and respond to our intuitive information cannot be stressed enough. It requires that we focus our attention on the moment as we gather information (reflection), decipher it and fashion a response (introspection), and then respond to our messages (integration). As an objective observer, we trust the message even when we do not understand it. For example: I act upon my intuition as long as my actions are not a danger to myself or another.

Sometimes our inner wisdom seems fragmented and incomprehensible. It may seem an impossible task to discern the meaning of each fragment and put the pieces together in an understandable way. We may relax into our intuitive awareness trusting that the potential meaning of the message rises to our consciousness. Through this awareness, we seek to discover the meaning inherent in the message. We may analyze the information or use free association to discover meaning. It doesn't matter how we discern; the mechanisms are not as important as the outcome: understanding the message.

RI^2 does not have to be a time-consuming practice. As we become skilled in using the process, we move more quickly through each step. For example: When I was training to be an intuitive, we were given a certain amount of time to reflect or gather information. Within the time limits there was little opportunity to question or doubt. I just trusted. It was only later that I might receive verification of my inner wisdom.

Intuition and the Four Aspects

We are holistic beings. Our inner wisdom speaks to us in all four aspects — body, mind, spirit, and heart. Paying attention to how the five primary facets interface with each aspect of our self helps us gain knowledge about the unique manner in which our intuition speaks. For example: I may find a heaviness in my body that I discount. I do not believe it is my intuition. Later, I may discover that the heaviness has nothing to do with my physical body; rather, it is grief speaking. My intuition is asking me to be with the grief in ways that allow me to release it and heal the resulting wounds.

Our inner wisdom impacts our physical body through our thoughts and emotions. The physical symptoms may draw us away from the message. Distracted, we are unable to recognize and respond to our intuition. When our emotions and thoughts distract us from the present moment, we lose our connection to our inner wisdom. This lost connection is not forever. With increased intuitive awareness, we identify mental and emotional barriers that impact our physical body. Through practice and experimentation, we deconstruct them. Each barrier we dismantle increases our intuitive awareness and our ability to respond to it accurately.

High emotions like anger, love, joy, and depression dull the connection to our senses by drawing us out of the moment. Being caught in a mental thought loop also impacts our awareness. If we obsess about something, we enter into a seemingly endless loop of rumination. We can move out of the loop by being awake, alert, and alive to our intuitive awareness. Our ability to effectively access our intuitive cues is unblocked.

No formula exists for enhanced intuitive awareness. In some moments, it is easier for us to recognize the voices of intuition. At other times, no matter how hard we try, entry into the facets may seem barred. Each moment of a3 awareness increases our ability to recognize and access our intuition. As we increase our capacity to identify, decipher, understand, and respond to intuitive nudges through the five primary facets, we move deeper into the five primary senses to explore their subtle nuances. These nuances are the fourteen secondary facets.

Chapter 6

Intuitive Sense: Secondary Facets

Through bare attention, our intuitive awareness flourishes. Moving from the mundane into the extraordinary through the between and back to the mundane, we become more attuned to how we gather and process our intuition. The more we focus on information gathered through our primary senses, the greater our awareness of how we gain information from the secondary facets will be.

Karen D. Olsen in Synergy: Transforming America's High Schools Through Integrated Thematic Instructions identifies nineteen senses. She begins with the five primary senses: sight, hearing, touch, smell, and taste. She further identifies another fourteen ways of accessing information. The additional fourteen are: balance, vestibular, temperature, pain, eidetic imagery, magnetic, infrared, ultraviolet, ionic, vomeronasal, proximal, electrical, barometric, and geogravimetric. These fourteen, for me, are secondary facets of the five primary intuitive sense facets. They are not independent senses; rather, they are subtle manifestations of the primary five. Each provides a more heightened way of accessing information.

Defining the Fourteen Secondary Facets

Balance: We are able to stay upright when we are walking or moving without being in a moving external environment like a vehicle, train, airplane. Although balance is a physical condition, it may manifest energetically. We may feel out of balance and question where in our life imbalance exists. Feelings of imbalance, mental/physical/emotional/ spiritual, are messages encouraging us to discover how we might return our four aspects, body, mind, spirit, and heart, to equilibrium.

If you are feeling out of balance, try cat walking: bend your knees slightly, and tuck your butt in. Allow your weight to rest on your thighs. Shift all your weight to the left leg. Step out with your right foot. As you place your right foot on the ground, roll from heel to toe until all your weight is on your right foot. Then move your left foot. As you place your left foot on the ground, roll from heel to toe until your entire foot is on the ground. Continue alternating feet. Open your senses, and allow your intuition to speak to you as you walk. Notice how you naturally move back into balance.

Vestibular: Our vestibular sense is another type of balance. This sense allows us to remain upright and stable when our external environment is moving. For example: we may be in a vehicle or dodging flying objects. When we are in tune with our intuition, our body responds by knowing exactly where to place our weight or shift our bodies.

Through our vestibular sense, we discover when stimuli in the external environment are impacting the balance of our emotions, mind, and spirit. For example: we may sense a misalignment in a relationship, financial records, or the words of another. We may have difficulty finding our footing in another aspect until we discover what is creating these feelings of imbalance.

Temperature: Most of us are able to sense temperature changes. We may flush, become lightheaded, sweat, or feel numb. While the temperature shift may be physical, it may also be sensed emotionally, mentally, and spiritually. Using our five primary senses, we gain additional information to use when deciphering the message.

For example: we may smell heat in the form of ozone or sulfur. We may shiver or sweat even if there is not a temperature change. We may sense vision distortions like a shimmering or a burst of light. Heat or cold may make snapping sounds, or we may taste the heat. Heat signatures alert us that there is something present that we are unable to clearly perceive in the mundane.

Pain: This is described in terms of a physical sensations, but may also be a phantom feeling triggered by our spirit, mind, or heart. No matter how it manifests, pain is a teacher. Even when what we are experiencing is physical, there is an intuitive message. For example: if we feel a sharp pain followed by the thought of a person or situation, the pain might represent emotions such as grief or sorrow.

Pain may also connect us to someone who is physically present. Empaths feel what is happening with another. We may feel the weight of their grief in our chest or get a phantom pain that mirrors theirs. The pain may also serve as a reminder to stop, slow down, and be aware of what is unfolding.

Eidetic imagery: Eidetic Imagery has been called photographic memory. Flashes of memory correspond to actions. For example: we think of a person, feel compelled to call them, and discover that they need our support. We might receive images of a place, an animal, or an object that provide an intuitive message. The eidetic imagery portal has helped me locate missing objects.

RI², (reflection, introspection, and integration) is particularly helpful in deciphering intuitive cues received from our eidetic imagery facet. For example: in reflection, we open to symbols. We may see a hawk and ponder its meaning. We use full-body listening to discover the image's impact. Next, through introspection, we use our logical mind to gain additional information including the energetic meaning of a hawk. Perhaps we see the hawk as a messenger and discover the answer to a question we have been pondering. During integration, we act upon the message.

Magnetic: Some of us are human magnets. Rather than walking around with metal stuck to us, our magnetic sense makes us a human compass who senses direction. This sense facet may draw us to a specific location. Although someone with a pronounced magnetic sense may not attract metal, they might be drawn to iron because they feel that the presence of iron enhances their intuitive abilities.

Our inner wisdom may prod us to look in a particular direction or travel to a certain destination. We may find our self poring over maps and then researching what lies in the direction we are drawn. We might access our magnetic sense through our senses of sight, hearing, and touch. What we are drawn to may necessitate that we explore further with other senses — both primary and secondary.

Infrared: Infrared and ultraviolet reside on opposite ends of the light spectrum just beyond visible light. An infrared light sensor measures the heat emanating from an object. The primary way to sense infrared is through touch, although intuitively we may notice it with our eyes. For example: wavy heat shimmers coming off of pavement are a form of infrared light.

Another way to sense infrared is with your eyes closed. Try this: with your eyes open, look intently at an object for about a minute. Then close your eyes. If you see a negative impression, a sepia background with yellowish images of what you saw with your eyes, you have accessed the infrared sense facet. Studying this negative image may provide additional information about the intuitive message.

Ultraviolet: Our ultraviolet sense provides information from light at the other end of the spectrum. Ultraviolet light is responsible for sunburns. For me, this facet provides information about higher nonphysical realms. I sense ultraviolet light as a pale light blue that is very cold. While I may not always physically sense the color, I do access it through the eidetic imagery facet. The coldness I feel is accessed through the temperature sense facet and the primary sense facet of touch.

When I sense ultraviolet light, it leads me to imbalances in the nonphysical aspects of the spirit, heart, and mind. Ultraviolet might also point to an imbalance in the physical world. As with all of our sense facets, the ultraviolet sense facet provides cues for responding to any aspect of our life.

Ionic: We use this facet to sense the displacement of particles. Ionic disturbances usually manifest as feelings of lightness, heaviness, flatness, or tingling. When we enter a room filled with joy and happiness, negative ions are present. We feel lighter. Conversely, when we are near grief, anger, or depression, the atmosphere seems heavy. Our bodies may feel sluggish or we may find it difficult to breathe. In either situation, we are reacting to the displacement of particles.

An empath easily feels the emotions of another. I believe they are sensitive to shifts from negative to positive ions. If an empath remains unaware of this intuitive sense facet, they continue to react and may experience fatigue. Anchoring and shielding are important practices for an empath. With these tools, they sense ionic shifts while minimizing the impact of them.

Vomeronasal: With this facet, we smell pheromones and respond to them. We unconsciously gain information about compatibility. We may meet someone and, without any logical reason, know they are someone who we want to befriend. The opposite is also true. We may meet someone and our intuitive alarms clang. We want to flee. These intuitive messages come from our vomeronasal sense facet.

We use the information from this facet in many ways. When we are unaware, we might not notice until much later that we understood the complexities of a situation but chose to ignore them. When hyperaware, we are better able to discern compatibility. We are more cautious and discerning in choosing work environments or social events.

For me, information gained from this sense has been the most difficult to accept. Often instead of trusting my inner knowing, I will judge it or myself critically. Only later do I discover why a person cannot be a friend or discover the pitfalls of a work environment. By listening to and accepting information from my vomeronasal sense, I make better choices.

Proximal: A shiver down the spine is a sign from our proximal sense. We may sense someone coming into a room or sneaking up on us even when we cannot hear or see them. Our skin may prickle. We notice things not discernible by our primary intuitive sense facets. Our proximal sense, nestled in the touch facet, is responsible for these reactions.

For example: we may smell roses when there are no roses near. Using RI2 we decipher the message within the smell of the roses. For me, a smell often reminds me of someone. If they are alive, I contact them. If they are deceased, I open to a message coming from that memory. Either way, I open myself to what my intuition is saying.

Electrical: The electrical sense activates when we feel current. We are aware of energy as it flows through our body. Hair standing up on our arms or feeling a zap of electricity when we touch someone are examples of receiving information from the electrical facet. This facet is similar to proximal. We sense energy shifts. But unlike proximal, we may actually touch something to access this facet.

For me, the electrical sense facet provides clues as to the emotional state of another. For example: individuals who have been diagnosed with certain mental illnesses carry specific energy signatures that resonate uncomfortably within me. Over time, I noticed that electrical and proximal facets often provide the same information in different ways. Either may amplify the other. The electrical facet is also used in conjunction with barometric.

Barometric: Barometric sensing is the ability to notice pressure changes. Individuals with previously broken bones or arthritic joints can accurately predict weather changes. They sense the barometric pressure change in their mended bones or arthritic joints. Barometric sensing may also manifest as a pressure in our ears or sinuses. I have sensed a prickling in my skin during shifts in pressure.

The barometric sense pairs with the primary touch facet and with the secondary proximal facet. For example: sensing the emotional density in a room may involve barometric, proximal, and vomeronasal facets. Try this: in an environment of heavy emotions, see how many of your sense facets provide information and how they verify your barometric sense.

Geogravimetric: The geogravimetric sense facet allows us to discern differences in size, mass, and density of objects. For example: a friend could look at a brochure layout and tell if it was an 1/8" out of alignment. Others may not need to measure ingredients when cooking. Have you ever just known something wasn't right without being able to identify what was wrong? If so, your information was accessed at least partially through the geogravimetric sense.

This sense helps us recognize what is out of alignment. The difference may not always be physical. The imbalance may manifest physically, emotionally, mentally, or spiritually. When something feels out of balance, ask yourself what that difference looks like. Another way to improve your skill with this sense is to consciously identify geogravimetric differences throughout your day.

All of us, to a certain extent, receive information from all nineteen intuitive sense facets. Practicing accessing information from each provides insights about how we receive information. By experimenting with identifying information from these facets, we gain a greater understanding of how we uniquely access our intuitive wisdom. When we are aware of this information, we are better able to identify the intent of the message.

As with most things, practice increases our intuitive ability. Each time we identify the intuitive cue and its facet of origin, we receive confirmation of our ability and gain confidence. We accept that we do know what we know without knowing how we know it. In time, we trust that we are intuitive even if we cannot prove the validity of our knowing.

Practicing accessing the secondary facets increases our ability to consciously move amid the mundane, extraordinary, and between. Our world is no longer experienced with, and contained by, what we understand through the five primary senses. We expand our perception through consciously accessing all nineteen intuitive sense facets. We enter the realm of the extraordinary through each of them. Connected to the source of our intuition, we become an incubator of intuition.

Aware of how our intuition manifests through the nineteen intuitive sense facets, we begin to recognize, on a conscious level, the many cues we had been gathering unconsciously. Each understanding of a message increases trust in our intuition. Open to our nineteen sense facets, we discover the subtleties of information that draw us deeper into the extraordinary.

Chapter 7

Intuitive Awareness & Intelligence

Much like our fingerprints, each of us has a unique way of accessing our inner wisdom. In our unique journey along the intuitive awareness continuum, we discover how we use each of our eight intelligences to process intuitive knowing. Using our intelligences, we identify our more easily accessed facets and create strategies to strengthen our ability to access others. Through our intuitive sense and our intelligences, we experience our intuitive nudges and act upon them. We reside in all three realms — the mundane, the between, and the extraordinary. We recognize our intuition is not a haphazard happening but an integral part of how we respond to the world around us.

Intuitive awareness is a right brain, left brain, across the corpus callosum, full-body way of gathering and deciphering information. Consciously and unconsciously we gather information using nineteen intuitive sense facets. With practice, we refine our ability to recognize how inner wisdom presents from each facet. Our world opens; our perception shifts. Our world becomes one of infinite possibilities as we notice the many ways our intuition manifests.

Accessing the facets and identifying intuitive cues are part of the initial stage of deciphering, understanding, and responding to our intuition. Using our intuitive processors, or our intelligences, we process the information. While IQ (intelligence quotient) helps us locate information, Emotional Intelligence (EI) outlined by Daniel Goleman, and Howard Gardner's eight intelligences: spatial/visual, kinesthetic/physical, musical/aural, linguistic/verbal, logical/mathematical, interpersonal/social, intrapersonal/solitary, and naturalistic, are instrumental in deciphering, understanding, and responding to our intuitive cues.

Use these intelligences to see past the mundane, peer into the extraordinary, and decipher intuitive messages in the between. IQ is the ability to obtain knowledge and differentiate between different types of knowledge. Emotional Intelligence is the ability to both identify emotions in others and minimize our reactions to those emotions. EI is the driver of our compassionate response. I call Gardner's intelligences intuitive sense processors. These power our response in the mundane. Once the message is identified with one of the nineteen intuitive sense facets and processed with one of Gardner's intelligences, we fashion a response using our Emotional Intelligence.

Intuition and Emotional Intelligence

The more proficient we become in accessing and processing our intuition, the better able we are to respond with our EI. Moving seamlessly between the triad realities and responding with EI takes practice. The goal of an intuitive is to be present in all three realms at the same time. It is important to remember that when we bridge the three, we align with our intuitive awareness.

By processing our intuitive nudges with our intelligences, we transform our reality. With our inner wisdom, we recognize the incongruity of our biases and judgments. When we listen to the truth as revealed through our intuition, our life aligns to our authentic self. Intuition becomes our guide to living authentically.

Intuition fuels each of our responses. When we receive an intuitive message, we choose, either consciously or unconsciously, to react or to respond to it. When we react, we are swept away by fear. Our EI is lowered. When we have a high EI, we are objective. We are aware of a trigger; we shift from reaction, and we respond intuitively.

We move along the intuitive continuum using our EI. Daniel Coleman identified five parts of Emotional Intelligence in his groundbreaking book by the same name. He stated that the hallmarks of EI were self-awareness, self-regulation, empathy, self-motivation, and effective relationship. Each component is necessary to our movement along the intuitive awareness continuum.

- Self-awareness is the foundation of intuitive awareness. As our inner wisdom manifests in each of our four aspects — body, mind, spirit, and heart — being awake and alert to our reactions leads to recognition of our intuitive cues. With self-awareness, we identify distractions and neutralize them. A3 awareness helps us develop self-awareness.

- Self-regulation helps us manage intuitive information and the way we receive it. Each of us has intuitive processing protocols. At times, we may spontaneously access our intelligences; in other moments, we are more deliberate in how we use them. Once information is deciphered, EI assists the management of our responses and increases our response flexibility.

- Empathy, our ability to sense emotions, is the power behind our intuitive awareness. When we are aware of the information received from empathy, we are able to objectively identify, decipher, understand, and respond to our inner wisdom. Empathetic awareness is our intuitive early warning system.

- Self-motivation ensures that we practice connecting to our intuition. In doing so, we gain the discipline to filter distractions from intuition. By motivating our self, we strengthen our connection to intuition and move along the intuitive awareness continuum.

- Effective relationships with our self, others, the Sacred, and all creation anchor us in the mundane and provide gateways to the extraordinary. This anchoring helps us differentiate between distractions and intuitive cues. Through these connections, we access collective wisdom, a receptacle of communal intuitive awareness.

Through our self-awareness and self-regulation, we process our intuitive nudges. Empathy powers our journey through the mundane, extraordinary, and between. The web we create through balanced relationships allows us to navigate through these three realms not as separate realities but as one cohesive world. Through the nineteen facets and our many intelligences, we navigate the uncertainty of the world with the power of our intuition.

As we become more proficient in processing our intuitive messages, we accept that there is no standardized test to measure intuitive awareness. We move along the intuitive awareness continuum recognizing that there are many ways of strengthening our connection to intuition. EI and the eight intelligences outlined by Howard Gardner are assets to processing intuitive information. (The eight intelligences are discussed in the next chapter.) For the purpose of this book, the eight intelligences are referred to as intuitive processors (IPs).

The way we access and process our intuition is as unique as our fingerprints. Although we do not need to understand the mechanics behind our intuitive awareness, this understanding is a way of increasing confidence. We may not be perfect in deciphering intuition, but as Bobby Robson said, "Practice makes permanent." We practice in order to discover which intelligences process information from our intuitive sense facets. We discern how to use our intelligences or intuitive processors to decipher our messages. I have found that the more I understand, the easier it is to make the triad realities my holistic reality.

If we cannot use one of our eight intuitive processors (IPs) today, that does not mean we will never be able to use it. As with all aspects of intuitive awareness, practice increases our ability to use not only that IP, but also to use others. Practice is vital. With practice, we discover which IPs are more easily used to process our intuition. Through practice, even the most fragile connection becomes stronger.

As we become more adept in recognizing how we process intuitive information using one intelligence, we can consciously process the same information using another IP. In doing so, we may gain additional information that brings greater clarity to the message while strengthening our ability to decipher using another intelligence.

Although it is easier to process information when we are aware, we need not be conscious of an intuitive cue in order to decipher and respond to it. At times, we may gain sudden clarity unaware of even how we received and processed the information. It may be only later that we put the pieces of the intuitive puzzle together. This happens more than you realize.

For example: During a meeting, I felt very clearly that we should not proceed with a project. Even though, on the surface, the project looked as if it would be a success, something felt off. Once we began to work on the project, we discovered that one team member had failed to disclose pertinent information. There was no way for me to know that something vital to the project had been withheld. I knew something was wrong, but I did not feel comfortable asking questions to uncover additional information.

(This is an example of gaining information from the proximal facet and processing it with social intelligence.)

Perhaps if I had spent time in reflection and introspection, I would have discovered what was amiss. Or, perhaps, I would have been more alert to ask questions that would have surfaced the missing information. Maybe I just didn't have the confidence to follow through with clarity seeking questions. No matter what I discovered in hindsight, this was a learning experience to not discount my intuition.

Being intuitive means being hyperaware, trusting your gut, and having confidence to decipher what you are feeling. Being an intuitive change agent requires that we are willing to learn from each experience by asking questions and thinking critically. We grow in our Emotional Intelligence and ability to process intuition by using our eight intelligences, which are discussed in the next chapter.

Chapter 8

Intuitive Intelligences as Intuitive Processors

Howard Gardner identified eight ways in which we learn. I refer to them as intuitive processors (IPs). They are spatial/visual, kinesthetic/physical, musical/aural, linguistic/verbal, logical/mathematical, interpersonal/social, intrapersonal/solitary, and naturalistic.

While Gardner's work is at the foundation of what follows, the information in this chapter is my understanding of how we process intuition. For me, using these intelligences is vital to deciphering intuitive cues. Do you need to know this information to respond to your intuition? No. Through the deconstruction of intuitive awareness components like intuitive sense facets and intuitive sense processors, we gain a better understanding of how we respond to our intuition and what hinders us from responding.

As with our ability to access certain intuitive sense facets, we more easily use certain IPs and struggle to process with others. Don't compare your capabilities with that of another or judge your abilities to process using a certain intelligence; rather, begin where you are by identifying which IPs you use more readily. Remember, practice makes permanent. Develop your ability to decipher with those IPs while exploring ways to increase your aptitude with others.

The Eight Intelligences or Intuitive Processors

Within each description, I weave the interactions of other intelligences with the one being defined. You may want to re-read this section once you gain an understanding of each intuitive processor to better understand these interactions.

Visual/Spatial Intelligence deciphers information using both physical eyes and our inner eyes. While our eyes might be drawn to a specific object like a bird, a rock, or a plant, we may see something internally like a memory or a flash image that activates this IP.

The visual/spatial intelligence connects the physical with three other aspects, mind/spirit/heart. We may objectively focus on a lost image and intuitively locate it through a flash image. We might receive a visual of a friend and feel compelled to contact them. Our visual IP helps us decipher cues received from visual-related intuitive sense facets and fashion the most appropriate response to them.

The spatial aspect of this IP enables us to identify what is out of the ordinary. For example: There may be an error on a spreadsheet. Becoming non-attached, our eyes are drawn to a part of the spreadsheet. We find the mistake. We may be able to identify structural defects, like mechanical problems, or notice someone's physical ailment. When processing spatially, we see beyond the physical or correlate the physical to our cue as we process information that we collected intuitively.

Try this: one way to strengthen the connection to this intelligence is to identify the images in 3-D drawings. In order for the picture to shift from two dimensional to three, soften your gaze by relaxing the muscles surrounding your eyes. While softening your gaze activates the visual IP, relaxing your muscles activates the kinesthetic IP, an intelligence discussed later.

Note that using two IPs concurrently results in enhanced intuitive awareness. Until we become more adept in recognizing information received concurrently from one or more of these facets, we may miss pieces of information necessary to gain a greater understanding of intuitive messages.

The visual/spatial IP requires full-body listening. With this practice we gain additional information. Through full-body listening we identify additional nuances and name how we received it. This enhances our ability to process the intuitive message.

For example: I may perceive congested energy near the heart chakra of someone. Through a conversation I discover the person is experiencing grief over the loss of a spouse. With this intuitive cue verified, I objectively seek additional clarity about the cue and process the information with my visual/spatial IP. My intuition guides me in an appropriate response.

Linguistic/Verbal Intelligence: Consciously and unconsciously we process information linguistically/verbally. Using this intelligence, we notice the nuances of both oral conversation and the written word. Our understanding of written messages increases when we combine this IP with others. For example: we gain greater understanding by listening to the melody of words with aural intelligence.

We process internally with this IP. Our thoughts have profound effects as they resonate through our four aspects. Words can be both beneficial and detrimental to our body, mind, spirit, and heart. Written and spoken, they can pierce our spirit. They have healing power as well. All words have the potential to reveal insights.

Linguistic intelligence requires that we feel the cadence and resonance of the words with our full-body. Using linguistic, aural, and kinesthetic IPs simultaneously increases our ability to interpret our intuitive nudges. Don't be overwhelmed by the thought of combining intelligences to discover the message of your intuition. You are already unconsciously using several as you decipher your intuitive messages.

Processing with this intelligence requires mindfulness. How often does what we hear or read trigger a reaction? When that happens to me, I step away from the words I hear or read. I ask myself what is being triggered. Only when I am objective do I gain clarity and am able to decipher the message.

It cannot be stressed enough that we cannot force intuitive understanding. We must be open to the many ways our intuition presents and the many opportunities we have to process it. Increasing our intuitive awareness comes through understanding the interconnectedness of our intelligences with one another that is vital to processing information gained through the nineteen intuitive sense facets.

Physical/Kinesthetic Intelligence is the processor of motion. Through movement our body becomes an antenna for information. Unless we are alert in the present moment, we may miss our body giving voice to our inner knowing. Even when we are mindful, we may ignore or negate messages.

We process the information with both gross and subtle movements. Writing may help us gain clarity. Walking or running may remove blocks to our inner wisdom as well. When we are comfortable with our body, we are better able to interpret the messages. For example: I use my kinesthetic intelligence through walking and journaling.

Loving and befriending our body increases our ability to interpret our inner wisdom using our kinesthetic intelligence. When we love and trust our body, we are more likely to recognize intuitive cues. Through hyperawareness we strengthen our connection to our body. No longer ignoring it, we are better able to respond in the ways our intuition guides us.

With physical intelligence we notice how our body reacts empathically to our emotions and those of another. These reactions are based on tension, anger, joy, or happiness emanating from a person or a group. Information processed through this intelligence may come from touch, vomeronasal, and proximal intuitive sense facets.

Kinesthetic intelligence processes cues available in all aspects of our self — body, mind, spirit, and heart. We experiment with this IP by noticing what information we are receiving from a sense facet, and then noticing how it presents in our body. For example: We may smell something with our vomeronasal sense, and our body prepares for flight. Instead of reacting, we note our trigger, decipher the message, and shift from reaction to response.

As we become increasingly more comfortable processing information physically, we have greater trust in what our body is telling us. For example: we feel a twinge in our lower back and identify what our body, mind, spirit, or heart is telling us. The more we know our body, the easier it is to discern if what we hear is a physical reaction, a distraction, or something to be intuitively deciphered.

When I am unable to identify a sensation as intuition or distraction, movement is one of the best ways for me to gain clarity. Walking, tai chi, and journaling help me process what my intuition is saying. As this movement frees my fear of not understanding, I am better able to decipher. Through movement, I attend to not only how I kinesthetically process what is happening, but also how my linguistic IP assists in the deciphering. It cannot be emphasized enough that we use multiple intelligences to understand our intuitive message.

Musical/Aural Intelligence: Our world is filled with natural and human made rhythms. With the aural IP, we gain intuitive understanding of these rhythms. Perhaps we process our intuition through the lyrics of a song or the wind rustling through the leaves. It may be the barking conversation between squirrels or the cawing dialogue of crows. Using this intelligence, we interpret the melodies of the world dancing around us.

This IP pairs with our kinesthetic IP as our body responds somatically to music. The sound resonates within our body; we physically process the information. Practicing bare attention, we listen to the dialogue between the aural and kinesthetic intelligences. Using this joint processing, we gain clarity of the message.

Music enters our being through many of our intuitive sense facets. While we most certainly hear it with our physical ears, we also recognize sound through the balance, vestibular, eidetic imagery, ionic, and electrical sense facets. We may even hear it through our proximal sense. Remember, you gain and process intuitive information in your own way. Explore how you process your intuitive whispers by feeling how they impact your being.

When beginning to explore processing with this intelligence, find a quiet place and enter into full-body listening. Use your primary senses to describe how the rhythm impacts you. Then notice what information you receive from other sense facets. Use your aural intelligence to sift through this information and discover the message.

For example: Intuitive awareness processing with my aural IP is often combined with another intelligence. I may pair the rhythm I am hearing with kinesthetic movement to receive greater understanding. Or, I may use my linguistic intelligence to discover what the lyrics to a particular song are saying to me intuitively.

Pairing aural intelligence with at least one other intelligence encourages a quicker deciphering of the message. For example: I hear a snippet of a song and then read the lyrics of the entire song. I use my aural and linguistic intelligences to process, understand, and form an appropriate response.

Logical/Mathematical Intelligence: Some believe that intuition is a right-brain ability that has no relationship to left-brain cognition. I do not believe this. Logic is as much a component of our intuitive awareness as our right brain functions. Intuitive awareness is a right brain, left brain, corpus callosum, full-body experience. When we listen with all our senses, our intuition presents. We process this information through all of our intelligences including our analytical and logical one.

Emotional Intelligence is not solely a right-brain endeavor. It is accessed through our entire body. EI removes reactive debris and distractions. It is foundational to our intuitive awareness. When our EI is high, we access our inner wisdom through all intuitive sense facets and process it with our logical/mathematical intelligence.

Using our logical/mathematical intelligence often results in creative, innovative response to intuition. When we focus our attention logically, we give our creative self space to evolve through its connection to our logical mind. The translation of the message occurs in the dynamic interaction of our creative and logical selves. Using this intelligence, we dissolve barriers between the creative and the logical. This illuminates a navigable pathway through the mundane into the extraordinary and the between.

Using logical/mathematical intelligence as an intuitive processor means accepting that intuition is a full-brain endeavor that opens us to possibilities. We recognize that some inner wisdom can only be deciphered using our mathematical intelligence. Patterns are one example. We may not understand the intuitive message of patterns without our logical IP.

We correlate what we are seeing with a root cause using this intelligence. For example: I remember the first time I became aware of the energetic impact of a physical fall. Using my third eye, I followed the skewed energy body and noticed how a person was laying on my massage table. In an epiphany moment, I saw the skewed energy body as a result of the physical fall.

Logic is a different but valid way of processing intuition. It could be argued that we use, to a certain extent, all nineteen sense facets when gathering information processed logically. For instance, if I play a game of solitaire or count my steps when walking, I disengage from my need to know. Focusing on logic problems creates a porous filter through which my processing seeps.

Interpersonal/Social Intelligence: The primary ways of processing our intuitive messages are interpersonal/social or intrapersonal/solitary. Many of us best process our intuition either with people or when we are alone. Just because it is easier to gain information in one of these two ways does not mean that we cannot become proficient in the other. Remember, we start where we are to move along the intuitive awareness continuum.

The interpersonal IP requires good personal boundaries, an awareness of empathetic reaction, and strong Emotional Intelligence. Using our social intelligence, we process inner wisdom through bi-listening. We attend to what cues were received internally while acknowledging any wisdom that manifests externally. We note what internal and external distractions prevent us from fully connecting to our intuition.

Bi-listening requires an environment of silence. Without silence, it would be difficult to gain clarity about what is occurring in the world while attending to our internal monologue. When we are with others, bi-listening to the internal and external worlds allows us to sift through distractions to find intuitive wisdom. We can choose to get lost in a crowd unaware, or we can hyperaware listen to others.

For those of us who need to cultivate interpersonal IP, I suggest spending time in a group without physically interacting. Focus on what is unfolding. In time, we develop the skills to interact with others while processing our intuitive knowing. Some do not need to develop this processor. They find it natural to process information socially.

As both an empath and an introvert, I have had to build good boundaries in order to use this IP. How did I acclimate to this intelligence? When I began to meet with clients, prior to the session, I would spend a significant amount of time energetically collecting information about my client and processing it. Now I seldom need to energetically connect prior to a session. The pre-work served as a primer to activate my social intelligence and to become more confident in my abilities.

As stated earlier, processing interpersonally requires hyperawareness of both internal monologue and external dialogue. The internal monologue provides feedback about distractions while emphasizing the message of our intuition. It is key to discriminate between them so that we are alert to where to focus our attention. The external dialogue provides intuitive clues or emphasizes what we intuitively know.

Social intelligence requires full engagement of our intuitive sense facets as we balance our internal understanding with external knowing. Through full-body listening, we identify how we acknowledge, respond, and react to the world. This is the foundation of processing interpersonally. We build upon this foundation by listening to what the other is saying and what is happening in our environment. Through bi-listening, we process the message, formulate a response, and articulate it.

Don't worry that you will miss what you need to know! Successfully engaging our social intelligence means interfacing with other intelligences. Think of social intelligence as a basket and the other intelligences as weaving through the bowl of processing. This information twines around in the bowl until one of our intelligences joins with it to process intuition.

Intrapersonal/Solitary Intelligence: If we find it easier to notice intuitive messages and process them when we are alone, then we are primarily intrapersonal/solitary processors. We process better in a controlled environment; we sift through the constant bombardment and filter distractions when we are alone. We identify not only the information but the particular intuitive sense facets they came from.

When we are alone, we can practice accessing information and processing it without interruption. Alone, we identify the many forms of our intuition: symbols, images, words, knowing without knowing how we received them. Once we identify the accessed information, we focus on the facets that brought us the information. Then, we decipher this wisdom using our intrapersonal intelligence combined with other intelligences.

As with our interpersonal intelligence, we do not use the intrapersonal IP alone. Walking or journaling (kinesthetic intelligence) triggers understanding. We may listen to music (aural intelligence) or process image memories (visual intelligence). Without the noise of distractions from others, it may be easier to identify, decipher, understand, and respond.

Our Interpersonal Intelligence processes information from any of the nineteen sense facets. We may choose to place filters on certain senses during the initial attempts at hyperawareness. For example: we may blindfold our self while focusing on touch. We may ignore our sense of smell and choosing instead to focus on the many ways we receive cues visually.

On the other hand, we may choose to open the floodgates of information and notice, without filters or expectations, what is incoming and where it comes from. No matter how we choose to experience our intuition when alone, we can practice accessing and processing our intuition without interference.

As with all intelligences, there are no rules for accessing information through our solitary intelligence. The goal is to immerse our self in sensory stimuli and notice without expectation. Through practice, we increase our intuitive awareness with this processor. It is that simple. There are no tests or grades. When we befriend intuition, we open our self to another way of being. This way of accessing and processing is unique to each of us. Remember the goal is not to be perfect; practice does make permanent.

Naturalistic Intelligence: Through the eighth intuitive processor we gain understanding through the natural world. Perhaps we notice squirrels scampering in trees or a cardinal perched on a fence and decipher the message. We find the meaning of natural symbols or identify feelings they engender. We leave the world of human-made constructs and shift our awareness fully into nature.

Through this IP, we are more fully engaged in the extraordinary. Spending time in nature opens a pathway to the extraordinary. For example: I remember the first time I went in search of wild mushrooms. When I finally found one, I saw many hiding in plain sight. I never looked at nature the same way again.

When processing our intuitive nudges with our naturalistic intelligence, we understand how deeply we are connected to the earth. Through this connection, we relate to others or circumstances in our life more dynamically. Nature gives us the opportunity to respond and react much differently than in a human constructed environment.

Books like Ted Andrew's Nature Speak and Animal-Speak provide deeper insights about the natural world. Through the information within them, we expand our awareness of the messages within the natural world and our ability to process our intuition through it.

All nineteen intuitive sense facets come alive in nature. Facets like barometric, geogravimetric , temperature, and magnetic are natural access points to engage nature and increase our intuitive awareness. We use our naturalistic intelligence to gain clarity about what we sense and how we respond to the world.

Strengthening Intuitive Awareness with the Eight Intelligences

Through the conscious use of our eight intelligences, we move along the intuitive awareness continuum. As our ability to process intuitive clues increases, our connection to inner wisdom grows. Although we receive intuition through our nineteen intuitive sense facets, our understanding takes shape through the use of our eight intelligences and our Emotional Intelligence. Hyperawareness increases the likelihood that we do not miss the intuitive nudges or opportunities to understand the message inherent in them.

Through the practice of RI², we reflect, introspect, and integrate as we bring meaning to these messages. Developing an environment of silence, we hear with clarity the whispers. We process the information gained. Through a foundation of silence and a practice of RI2, we use our intuitive processors to gain greater access to our intuition. We identify, decipher, understand, and respond to our intuition.

Building a foundation of meditation, petition, and contemplation moves us along the intuitive awareness continuum. With increased confidence, we trust what we receive intuitively. We gain confidence in our abilities. We accept that we are intuitive. Creating filters and recognizing the difference between distractions and intuitive nudges becomes more important as we take the next step along the intuitive awareness continuum. That step? Maintaining the stance of the objective observer.

Chapter 9

Intuitive Presence

We are all intuitive. This is an indisputable fact. For some, living from their intuitive abilities is as natural as breathing. For others, blocks, including fear, prevent them from engaging their intuitive nature. We all get stuck at some point; practice is the way to dissolving barriers and recognizing the voice of intuition. The more we practice connecting to our inner wisdom, the greater our confidence in our abilities. Through practice, we develop our intuitive presence; we trust that we hear our intuition.

Intuitive Presence

We cultivate our intuitive presence through each moment spent being aware of the interconnectedness of the triad realities. In this state of heightened awareness, the world appears more. To stay in this moment, we focus both internally and externally. We are fully engaged in everything — when we drive, we drive; when we cook, we cook; when we meditate, we meditate. Within intuitive presence, we no longer walk between three worlds; we live simultaneously in the mundane, the extraordinary, and the between.

How do we develop and sustain intuitive presence? With hyperawareness gained through anchoring and shielding. Hyperawareness, a state in which we sense with clarity, occurs when we are anchored in the moment and shielded from distractions. Unanchored from the moment, we are unable to filter distractions. We may sense deeply what is occurring, but we get caught in emotional and mental distractions. Being caught need not be a permanent condition.

Anchoring and Shielding

Through anchoring and shielding we create the foundation for navigating through distractions and identifying intuitive cues. In this state of hyperawareness, we create a connection from our internal to external worlds. We ensure that we are not a closed circuit. In fact through our connections, we experience the moment in meaningful, interconnected ways.

Anchored, we are present to what is happening. We connect all four aspects — body, mind, spirit, and heart — through our spirit thread. All living beings have these four aspects that integrate with universal aspects. This integration or connection occurs through our spirit. The universal collective has four aspects as well — body, mind, spirit, and heart. We intentionally connect to the universal aspects within the repository of intuitive knowing. Through this connection, we gain clarity.

Anchoring or grounding into the moment may be an elaborate process, or it may be a simple, quick way to reaffirm our connection. There is no wrong way to anchor into the moment. A simple way to anchor begins by focusing on the breath. Try this: do not shift your breathing, but attend to its cadence, allowing the rhythm of your breath to sync with the rhythm of the earth and source.

Anchoring and shielding can also be attained through a longer meditative practice. Try this: visualize a bright light entering through your crown. With each successive breath, pull the light further into your body. Feel yourself physically relaxing, your emotions calming, your thoughts quieting. As the light draws deeper into your body, feel your body/mind/spirit/heart aligning. The light continues its journey downward through your torso, into both of your legs, past your knees, through your ankles, and out the soles of your feet. This light twining with your light grows roots into the earth. Feel your connection to the earth as your energy, earth energy, and source energy weave together.

Rest in this connection. When you are ready, begin to gently draw up this mingled essence through your body with each inhale. The breath follows a reverse path upward. Visualizing the three twined essences moving up your body through your legs, torso, neck, head, out the crown. As this braid travels upward out of your body, feel it exit your crown and travel toward Source. Connect with the source of all as you visualize branches expanding around you and leaves unfurling. Feel the braid's energy expand into this unfurling. Notice how it connects you to all and shields you from distractions.

Three separate strands — source, self, and earth — weave together as they consciously connect to the Source. With this connection, the anchor is complete, and the circuit of connection activated. The braid is energized as we breathe through this connection of earth, source, and self-essences. Hyperaware, we are alert for the voice of intuition.

Through anchoring and shielding, we create filters through which we sift information. Although the bombardment upon our intuitive sense does not lessen, we are better able to differentiate between distractions and intuitive nudges. Using our intuitive processors, we decipher the information, and we integrate it into our responses. Each time we identify, decipher, understand and respond to our intuition, our anchor and shield strengthen.

We know what we know because anchoring connects us to our foundation of objectivity. Anchored, we listen to our internal monologue in a different way. It is an early warning system that notifies us when we make choices based upon assumptions, judgments, or defenses. We notice when we are attaching or detaching. Anchored, we objectively choose not to react. Instead we use our intuition to respond.

With shielding comes clarity. When we are shielded, we recognize the potential of being hooked by our judgments. We recognize how we are caught in our desire to defend. We identify the violence inherent in inner thoughts, words, and actions. As we discard our distractions, we use the power of our intuition to avoid reactive behavior. We choose intuitive presence.

Living in intuitive presence does not mean we are never caught by our triggers; rather, we acknowledge what hooks us. While intuitive abilities are not perfect and we occasionally get caught, we are aware of intuition's guiding power. We learn from each experience no matter if we received an intuition message or were distracted. We note how distractions get in the way of identifying, deciphering, understanding, and responding to our intuition.

Anchoring is foundational to remaining objective and open to our intuition. Initially, we consciously anchor. In time, being anchored is our natural resting state. Anchored, we forge a pathway of intuitive focus in every moment. Intuition guides us on the ongoing journey to be our most authentic self. As long as we live, we learn, evolve, and grow in intuitive awareness.

Intuitive Awareness and Synaptic Pruning

We are amazing creatures. As we learn new habits, we intuitively let go of others. We deepen our intuitive presence through a process is called synaptic pruning. Neural synapses that are no longer needed are pruned by responding to our intuition. As old patterns are discarded, we create new patterns of thoughts and actions. Another way to view this is that when our path forks and we choose to follow one branch, the other fork becomes overgrown and impassable with disuse. In other words, when we no longer engage in a habit over a period of time, it becomes more difficult to access.

As we move along the intuitive awareness continuum, synaptic pruning is an important tool. We follow the pathways that lead us to our intuitive knowing. We choose what habits to strengthen. When we choose to follow the paths that lead to our authentic self, we better identify, decipher, understand, and respond to our intuitive messages.

No matter how connected we are to our authentic self and no matter how far along the intuitive awareness continuum we are, we may still find it difficult to separate intuitive cues from distractions. In those moments of confusion, we anchor and shield. Connection revitalized, the fog around our intuitive sense clears. Anchored and shielded, it is easier to participate in full-body listening. Through full-body listening, we identify intuitive cues and objectively decipher the message.

The Intuitive Collection with Full-Body Listening

Through full-body listening, we follow the pathway of our intuition as it flows across our corpus callosum connecting our right and left brains. Using our intuitive sense facets, we collect information from all aspects of our self. We decipher potential meanings obtained through our intuitive sense using our intelligences. We consciously use the intuitive triad of meditation, petition, and contemplation.

We recognize that what we do not understand has the power to be misinterpreted when we focus our awareness, state our intent, and listen to intuition's voice. But, we cannot let fear of misinterpretation stand in our way. Fear is the ultimate shenpa. When it catches us, the extraordinary becomes obscured. Instead of gaining clarity, our fear-filled reactions create illusions. We are unable to accurately identify our intuitive nudges much less understand them. Recognizing that we are stuck, we reconnect to our intuitive awareness through anchoring.

Reconnection boosts our ability to see clearly. We recognize fear-filled performance anxiety. We may desperately want to know the intuitive answer for we believe this knowledge will resolve our challenges. But as with all fears, performance anxiety may lead to false positives. We may believe that we understand the message. We may not. Acknowledging our fear may not diminish these feelings; this recognition makes us alert to how it distracts us.

Fear alerts us to the potential of misinterpretations. Please note, there is no shame in misinterpreting our intuition. It is a learning experience that nudges us back onto our intuitive path. Through practice, we learn to harness the power of our intuitive awareness even if we are filled with fear. Through practice, we become less a fear sieve through which information indiscriminately flows and more an objective observer who separates intuition from distractions.

Balancing Doing With Being

To foster our intuitive presence, we balance doing with being. Being, for me, is a means of integrating all four aspects of self — body, mind, spirit, heart — in ways that form intent. Doing is an expression of intent. We energize our hyperawareness through being and doing or through intent and action. Both are important aspects of living in intuitive presence.

Our doing propels us through our life. By connecting our being and doing, we enter the extraordinary. Within this connection, we explore what is preventing us from listening intuitively. We identify barriers and dismantle them. As our being and doing connect, we form the bridge from intuitive message to response.

Within intuitive presence, our doing aligns with our being. Being is who we are authentically. Doing is our outward authentic expression of self. When our being represents our core intent, doing is a natural result. Through their alignment, we are better able to identify, understand, and respond to our intuition. We respond with the guidance of intuition. Our life becomes an expression of our soul purpose.

Internal Monologue Awareness

In intuitive presence, we continually look for ways to increase self-awareness. We regularly engage in full-body listening to discern how and why we respond or react to the world. We listen to our internal monologue. We gain a greater intuitive understanding of how our perceptions create our reality and discern how inaccurate perceptions are the basis of our illusions.

By attending to our internal monologue, we become aware of threats to our intuitive presence. The four aspects of the self speak through our internal monologue, providing information about what prevents us from connecting to our intuition. With this knowledge, we gain the ability to dissolve barriers to our inner wisdom.

Intuition and Soul Purpose

With the barriers dissolved, we intuitively connect to our soul purpose. Even in those moments when we do not understand, we trust and are confident in our abilities. For example: when intuition is unclear, I listen to discern its validity. Next, I decipher the message using my intelligences. Only after this discernment do I choose how to respond to the information. This response may be to ignore a distraction, respond immediately to the message, or to wait to respond. If I am still unsure, I ask myself if responding to my intuition will result in harm to myself or another. If the answer is "no," I act upon my intuition.

The process of identifying, deciphering, understanding, and responding to intuition may happen in as little as several seconds or as long as years. We understand the message of our intuition when we need to respond to it. As acceptance increases our confidence, the connection to our intuition becomes easier. Our deciphering grows in accuracy.

Trust in our intuitive ability is important as we move along the intuitive awareness continuum. Becoming progressively aware of our intuition depends upon whether or not we believe in our intuitive abilities. The more we practice, the better able we are to identify how intuition speaks to us and how we decipher the message. While practice does not make perfect, it does prepare us to navigate through life using our intuitive awareness. With confidence and trust, we clearly see the accuracy of our inner knowing. Our intuitive presence grows.

Chapter 10

Walking Amid the Triad Realities

Maybe you have been there — teetering on the threshold of the extraordinary. You identify an intuitive cue, but struggle to decipher its message. The more you focus on the clue, the farther it slips from the moment. You spiral into frustration. Distractions overwhelm. You are unable to identify the message much less move into the between to decipher it and fashion a response.

If this resonates with you, you are not alone. Each of us has experienced the frustration of not being able to identify an intuitive message. Our world is awash with distractions. To successfully pluck intuitive messages from the extraordinary, we cultivate an environment of silence. Here we lessen the white noise of distraction. We open our self to clarity. This may mean disengaging from the frenetic pace of the moment and consciously documenting suspected cues.

If we can, we discern the intuitive message when we receive it. But, it is perfectly okay to wait to decipher it. The key is to have a clear mind when deciphering intuition. When we experience moments of diminished clarity and clouded intuitive vision, we clear our mind by anchoring and shielding. Becoming fully present in the moment, we are able to perceive what the extraordinary is sharing.

The farther we move along the intuitive awareness continuum, the greater the urgency we feel to stop sleepwalking through life. We consciously practice a3 awareness. Eagerly awake to each moment, we are alert to our intuitive cues. We are alive to their identification, deciphering, and understanding. By fully focusing on the moment, our inner wisdom seems to fly from our intuitive sense facets. We act upon its messages.

Important intuitive messages are never lost. They speak to us from different facets until we have no choice but to hear them. For example: we may notice the same topic surfacing in conversations, showing up on social media feeds or in the news. Our dreams replay the same subject until we listen. We may see the same animal. At some point, we recognize the intuitive thread. We discern the message.

The Triad Realities

Although the extraordinary is the origin of our intuition, each of the three realities has a specific purpose. Walking amid the worlds, we identify our nudges in the extraordinary, process them in the between, and return to the mundane to act upon the messages. Learning to move seamlessly through each realm enhances our intuitive awareness. With increasingly greater duration, an intuitive exists in all worlds simultaneously.

Crossing the threshold of each world requires focusing our attention on the present moment. A focused intuitive is an anchored intuitive. Nonattached and hyperaware, we trust that our intuition draws us to what we need. For example: we may engage a friend in conversation with, notice a mistake on a spreadsheet, or respond to a nudge to turn right instead of left when driving. We intentionally sift through each piece of intuitive information by reflecting and introspecting.

As we gain experience moving amid the three realms, we are better able to discern what is authentic and what is an illusion. As we identify the illusions that catch us, we use our inner wisdom to discern the root of a particular illusion. Unmasking illusion is the final barrier to the extraordinary. Once removed, we peer with clear sight into the extraordinary. Using the information gained while in the extraordinary, we process the messages using our intelligences.

Unless we are mindfully present, we may react to messages of distraction present in our thoughts, words, and emotions. We may judge, excuse, and make assumptions while we intellectualize, analyze, and attempt to find logical reasons for everything. We get stuck in the belief that if we can "prove" it, then it exists. If it cannot be "proven," it is not real. This attitude blocks our connection to intuition.

RI²: Deciphering Our Intuition

As we move along the intuitive awareness continuum, we open to how we get trapped. Instead of reacting to triggers, we seek the message inherent in each. Then we reflect and introspect to find its meaning. These two parts of RI² may happen spontaneously, or we may need time in silence to gain understanding. Realize that it does not matter how we access the intuitive message; deciphering, understanding, and responding to our intuitive messages is what matters.

While both our analytical and creative minds are necessary to decipher our intuition, we begin in the creative mind with reflection. During this mindful activity, we notice without judging or defending. Through full-body listening we gain information not only about the stimulus, but also our initial reactions and responses.

Through reflection, the beats of our intuition synchronize with the rhythm of our hearts. We gain information. Our heart aspect is our intuitive awareness powerhouse. Within this aspect resides quiet noticing, acceptance, and non-judgment. Nudges are often first recognized here. By identifying and understanding our emotions and their roots, we notice subtle cues speaking through our other aspects — body, mind, and spirit.

We need not know the why of intuition; we need only trust that we know. There is little logic in the heart aspect. We accept the intuitive message and trust it will make sense at some point. During reflection, we trust without logically verifying. With each verified message we gain confidence in our abilities. As we move along the intuitive awareness continuum, our intuitive presence expands.

While trusting what we are sensing might be easier when operating from the heart, so is reacting to distractions. Experiencing from the heart is best accomplished objectively. While gathering information is a heart-centered task, we open to the flood of sensations without naming or judging. This gathering is accomplished in silence, an environment in which we mindfully engage the connection of our right and left brains through the corpus callosum.

Using our intuitive sense facets, we sift through information as we separate illusions and distractions from intuition. Then, we move from the heart to the head. Through introspection, we process our intuition with our mind aspect. Introspection is both a right- and left-brain function experienced through the corpus callosum. We connect to our intuition through both creativity and logic. In doing so, our connection to intuitive understanding is strengthened.

Intuition and Our Nervous System

Accessing our intuitive awareness occurs on both sides of the brain. Information gained in the right and left brains converge in the corpus callosum, the bridge between the two hemispheres. Intuitive awareness is a holistic experience that happens in our corpus callosum.

Our nervous system is an energy system. Within the synapses of our nervous system all three realities — mundane, between, extraordinary — converge. We recognize our intuition, process the information, and choose how to respond. As the synapses fire in the corpus callosum, we gain clarity. I believe that we process our inner knowing with the synaptic connections of our nervous system. Again, I believe this processing is strongest in the corpus callosum.

If we accept that intuitive awareness is a corpus callosum activity, the right vs. left brain argument is inconsequential. No longer does someone need to identify as right brained to be considered intuitive. If we accept that intuition is a product of both hemispheres of the brain and the corpus callosum, it follows that everyone is intuitive. Intuition is as likely to manifest as emotional and creative as it is logical, rational, and analytical. With this paradigm shift, we open to accessing and processing our inner knowing in limitless ways.

For example: when I am walking, the crispness of the air or a flying hawk may trigger my intuition. Likewise, when I am working on a spreadsheet and have no clue why it is out of balance, my eyes might be drawn to the very place of error. Relaxing into the moment in both situations allows my intuitive knowing to surface in whatever way I need. Letting go of my want to know helps me become more receptive to my intuition.

Intuitive awareness does not exist in a world defined by labels, rules, and definitions. Our unique inner knowing is flexible and dynamic. Just when we have figured out how we access intuition, we discover new ways to hear the voices of our intuition. When we are open to the dynamic nature of our intuition, we receive information that doesn't fit within carefully defined parameters. Accepting that intuition is organic and flexible empowers us to become more aware and accepting of our intuition.

Being comfortable with our intuitive nature may be a difficult adjustment. If distractions prevent us from being mindfully aware, we become overwhelmed. Seeing clearly seems impossible. Paralyzed, we fear inaccurately categorizing information as inner wisdom or distraction. We are unable to separate truth from illusion.

At this point we may unconsciously step back into the mundane, closing our eyes to the extraordinary. We lose access to the between. Disregarding our inner knowing is not the answer. Mindfulness is. A mindfulness practice such as focusing on the breath anchors us into the moment. Being present illuminates the path of our intuition. Reconnected, we move forward with curious daring and courage.

Shielding

As we grow more adept in accessing and processing our intuitive awareness, shielding becomes an increasingly more important mindfulness practice. Shielding creates a permeable barrier between us and the world. This filter enhances our awareness of intuition and distractions. Through it we recognize our triggers and take steps to prevent reactions. Shielding does not prevent us from interacting with others; rather, this protective barrier allows us to intentionally filter what we are receiving.

Shielding is both an early warning system and an internal guidance system. It alerts us to distractions. It provides insight about where to focus our attention. For example: I may feel my body tensing. This may be followed by a headache or anxiety. When I look for the cause of these symptoms, it may be a fear manifesting or my intuition telling me that I need to pay attention. By focusing my attention, I objectively rise above the tumult to engage my intuition.

Creating a shield begins in silence. This is not a cessation of noise but a place of increased clarity. Within it, we discern the difference between distractions and intuitive nudges. This discernment is vital to maintaining the shield's integrity. We do not just put up a shield and never tend to it. Each action either ensures its cohesion or contributes to its deterioration.

If we are with a person or in a situation that is toxic, not listening to our intuitive messages erodes the shield. When in sync with the intuitive messages that ping our shield, we recognize barriers to deciphering and responding to our intuition. With this recognition, we enable our intuition to guide us in our response formulation. Simply put, we remove ourselves from the situation.

As with anchoring, the shield serves as another defense against distractions. It is used in conjunction with anchoring and other tools. Realize that none of these tools are magical. They help us focus our attention in the moment. Being present, we note how illusion and distractions impact us. We use the tools to awaken all four aspects — body, mind, spirit, and heart. Awake, we release the illusions.

Our breath balances us and prepares our body, mind, spirit, and heart for the shield. Each inhale contains the breath behind the breath or "ruah." Hebrew for spirit or animator, ruah has been referred to as the Holy Spirit in Christianity, prana in Hinduism, qi by the Chinese, and ha by Hawaiians. The breath behind the breath is a metaphor for the presence of the Sacred in each moment. Ruah helps form the permeable barrier and raises our intuitive awareness through its connection to the extraordinary. Intuition rides upon this breath.

In order to shield our self, being aware and objective is vital. We begin by anchoring our self and then returning to our breath. (See the meditation for anchoring in previous chapter.) Through our breath, we gain a greater understanding of where distractions are most likely to occur and how they alert us to their presence.

This shield does not shut people or the world out. It is a gentle buffer that slows down the bombardment while helping us remain in the present moment. The shield is not magical; rather, it is a focuser of our intent. With it, we are more firmly anchored in the moment. The shield is a tool of awareness — nothing more, nothing less.

When we are shielded, we more easily recognize opportunities to enter the extraordinary and explore our intuition. Through this permeable bubble, we focus our inner vision. It is like binoculars for all of our intuitive sense facets. Shielding is a way of sensitizing the four aspects of our self to the extraordinary. The distractions as well as intuition are more pronounced through the lens of our shield. We change our consciousness at will to identify the message.

An example: Instead of looking at autumn as a time of dying and loss, we may look at it as a way of perceiving what remains when the world is stripped bare. As we near winter, we can see what lays hidden during the summer and early fall. In these moments, the extraordinary invites us to see beyond the superficial and peer into the world of intuitive messaging.

One fall, I gave a retreat at the Sisters of Charity of Cincinnati. I walked the grounds snapping photos with my phone. My intent was to capture the beauty of the grounds. Once back in my room, I reviewed the images. One of the trees, shorn of all its leaves, looked like a slender woman with her hands lifted to the sky in joy. Her head appeared as part of the trunk. That head was turned toward me.

Using the three-step process of meditation/petition/contemplation, I felt the woman of the tree inviting me to experience her joy as she stood on a bluff overlooking the Ohio River. As I deciphered this image, the tree became a symbol for my own life. Even though I was in a dark period, filled with much anxiety and disappointment, joy was ever-present. I had only to open my eyes to feel the joy hidden beneath what appeared barren. Using the intuitive cues as a prompt, my intelligences processed the information. I felt joy in all four aspects of my being.

Crossing the threshold into the extraordinary requires intention, preparation, and trust. Being shieldless doesn't mean that we will not hear our intuition; it just means its entry may be more tumultuous and our ability to identify and recognize its messages greatly diminished. We may lack sufficient expertise to adequately decipher the message. With practice, we notice any disconnect, shield and anchor, and return to the moment.

As we rest in the silence, our ability to recognize the intuitive nudges increases. Accessing our intuition occurs with greater frequency. We return to our natural state — being intuitively aware. By grounding and shielding, we further strengthen our intuitive abilities. We hear our intuitive nudges with greater clarity. We process and respond to them with greater frequency.

Although it is impossible to be 100 percent prepared for incoming intuitive nudges, with practice, we are more likely to recognize the whispers and use meditation/petition/contemplation to decipher them. Identifying, recognizing, understanding, and responding to our intuition is only possible through full-body listening. This way of sensing is more easily accessed when we ground and shield.

Chapter 11

Intuitive Awareness As Experiential Awareness

Please note that to fully engage our intuition, we must have both internal and external engaged listening. Internal engaged listening is attending to our internal monologue speaking through all four aspects of self. External engaged listening includes an awareness of exterior distractions and how they create barriers to accessing intuition. An external distraction could be inclement weather, traffic or the crying of a child.

Intuitive awareness is experiential awareness. It is a full-body, all-aspect way of living. When we engage life in this way, intuition becomes our internal GPS. We gain information through the nineteen intuitive sense facets and use our eight intelligences to process it. The intelligences and intuitive sense facets are not separate; through them we identify, decipher, understand, and respond to our intuition.

Engaged listening is all access noticing. Through it we discover the best ways to remove the barriers of distraction and illusion that prevent our connecting to our intuition. For me, engaged listening includes walking, journaling, or focusing on my breath while intentionally relaxing. When relaxed, I am more objective, more mindful. The more mindful I am, the greater the recognition of my intuition.

The Practice of Meditatio/Oratio/Contemplatio

Engaged listening requires the practice of meditatio/oratio/contemplatio. This intuitive triad is the part of engaged listening that is inward focused.

- Meditatio or meditation is a means of focusing attention on the extraordinary. By focusing our attention through meditatio, we identify messages.

- Oratio is the forming of intent, or a petition, to understand what is unfolding. In oratio, we intend to understand the message of our intuition.

- Contemplatio is actively listening to our intuition. Contemplatio is the quiet listening that attunes us to the messages of intuition.

Understanding what is impacting us externally is foundational to removing barriers and getting to the core of our intuitive message. As distractions are filtered, we clearly see how our intuition speaks to us. We open our self to however our intuition manifests. There is no formula for receiving intuition; we trust that our intuition guides us. We recognize that everything has the potential to hold an intuitive message. Through intentional listening, the messages are identified.

Engaged Listening

Engaged listening means befriending our body. Every time we stop, breathe, and notice the sensations in our body/mind/spirit/heart, we connect with our self. We may notice aches and pains and focus on discovering physical, mental, emotional, and spiritual roots of misalignment. The more we befriend our bodies, the better able we are to discern what is stopping us from listening and responding to our intuition.

Our bodies have much to share intuitively. If we are not loving, gentle, and kind to our body, it remains in a state of high alert. Fight or flight becomes our modus operandi. We get fatigued. The way out of fatigue into intuitive awareness is self-compassion. Self-compassion allows us to own any personal suffering and take steps to minimize it. Moving into a place of respite, we open to what our body is telling us.

As with all things intuitive, engaged listening requires practice. It is easy to get frustrated when those initial forays into this listening yield little or indecipherable information. When we listen with our entire body, we receive more than intuitive information. Engaged listening provides information about which aspects of self are out of balance as well as when our internal monologue is stuck in an endless loop of distraction.

Through engaged listening we gain clarity about which intuitive sense facets and intuitive processors are being more easily accessed. Try this: During an engaged listening practice session, identify the intuitive messages. Process them immediately. Name the intuitive sense facet and intelligence that was instrumental in your awareness.

Ask yourself if you noticed the cues when you were alone or when you were with others. How did you receive the cues? Maybe you were in nature or using your logical brain to make sense of the nudge. Maybe how you received or processed the information was surprising. There is no wrong way to receive intuitive information. Engaged listening opens us to where we are on the intuitive awareness continuum.

The Intuitive Awareness Continuum

Moving along the intuitive awareness continuum is a lifelong process that necessitates understanding our self. With each moment of intuitive awareness, we better understand our self. Walking amid the worlds of the mundane, extraordinary, and between becomes our new normal. The more we experience moving through these three realities, the easier it becomes to identify the intuitive knowing, decipher it, understand it, and respond with it. We let go of the illusions and become more fully our authentic self.

This all-aspect awareness deepens as we spend time in solitude. Regular time alone strengthens our ability to recognize intuition. Recognition is the first step to responding to our intuition. The more we practice accessing our intuition, the easier it is to enter this hyperaware state at any moment.

As we gain information, we see details and understand their importance to the whole. We grasp the bigger picture. For example: Making mistakes on a spreadsheet is easy when you are not mindful. It is inevitable that mistakes are made. If I allow myself to be overwhelmed by the task of locating mistakes, discovering them proves almost impossible. When I am hyperaware, my eyes are drawn to errors on a spreadsheet. This is a practical way of using intuition.

Schedule regular moments of silence. During this time, ask a question and notice how intuition manifests within the answer. Or, just notice which facets provide clues. For example: when the barometric pressure changes, my right inner ear begins to feel congested. I discover what a physical sensation was saying by asking myself what was happening externally.

We create moments of hyperawareness through meditatio, focusing our awareness on the extraordinary. Using meditatio, we intentionally listen to the voice of our intuition. We examine what catches our attention in all four aspects — mentally, emotionally, physically, and spiritually — while allowing our intuition to guide us. We do not have an agenda; rather, we focus in ways that bring a greater understanding to how we identify, decipher, and understand our intuition.

Each of us must discover how to maintain a state of hyperawareness. I describe entering this way of sensing as taking two steps back and sliding into awareness. For me, this means focusing on my breathing, identifying whatever angst I am feeling, and relaxing into the moment. With practice, I move fairly quickly through meditatio and oratio as I open myself to the quiet listening of contemplatio. While you might try what works for me, ultimately this is your path. Explore how to use your skill set to the best of your ability.

For me, contemplatio is a movement into intuitive awareness has discernible physiological changes. The muscles around my eyes relax. My vision softens; my hearing becomes more acute; I separate individual sounds from collective noise. I notice an internal shiver or feel physically lighter. I open to the many ways my intuitive sense facets draw my attention.

The way we experience a shift into intuitive awareness is as unique as our ability to access intuition. Moving along the intuitive awareness continuum can be less described than experienced. The intuitive sensations we experience are not static. What heralds inner wisdom today may not be the ways we experience it in the future. As we gain confidence and practice, we notice our intuitive messages in whatever way they manifest.

When we ask our self what is the foundation of what we are experiencing, we gain the answer by attending to our body, mind, spirit, and heart. For example: I use meditatio/oratio/contemplatio to discover the actual root of the angst. If the feeling is more heart centered, I open myself to deciphering my intuitive message. If my heart aspect is calm, the message is more often intuitive and not a distraction.

If you cannot tell if something is a distraction or intuitive, don't judge the cue. Move into deciphering. If it is a distraction, you will discover that as you seek to understand. As you seek clarity, you may realize additional information is needed. For example: a sparrow visited me for two weeks during Tai Chi sessions. The bird stayed within four feet of our practice space. I researched the meaning of a sparrow to get a better understanding of the message. The sparrow reminded me that no matter how many people attended my class that I should believe in my abilities.

The 4nons

What is discovered during deciphering and understanding helps us fashion a response. The practice of the 4nons — non-attachment, non-judgment, non-defended, and nonviolence —accentuate hyperaware-ness, the stance critical for deciphering and understanding. When non-attached, we release the pressure of wanting something to be true or false so badly that we cling to mistruths and push away information that would negate our point of view.

For example, during a recent relationship, my intuition clearly spoke. We were toxic to each other. I ignored all the warning signs. I re-acted to the distractions and ignored the intuitive cues. I created more illusions instead of responding with intuition. The relationship ended badly.

Engaged listening requires a non-judgmental, non-defensive stance. At times it may be impossible to describe why we know what we know. Our first instinct may be to judge the message as inaccurate or identify a distraction as intuition. We may want to defend our illusions. When we are intuitively aware, we recognize how our assumptions and judg-ments inhibit our intuitive knowing.

Embracing our intuitive awareness means that we trust that our body/mind/spirit/heart do not lie. We trust our ability. We do not have to defend what we know as truth. We are aware of the potential for per-formance anxiety. To reduce performance anxiety, we remind our self that if we respond to what we believe is intuition and cause no harm, it doesn't matter if we have misinterpreted the nudge.

If necessary, return to intuitive knowing and dissect it. For example: I ask myself, "how do I know what I know?" I engage in reflective en-gaged listening. I recall the message and notice through which sense or senses I accessed this knowledge. I identify how I process the informa-tion. Hindsight often provides greater clarity than foresight. Reflection is a tool that enhances the connection to our intuition.

When we focus using engaged listening, we need not loudly affirm what we know. There is no need to convince anyone else of our intuition. Even when it seems the message is for someone else, we do not blurt it out. We share it as a response to their words or actions. We realize that our intuition guides our journey and may be inappropriate to share with another.

Engaged listening is a stance that increases intuitive awareness. The more we practice, the more refined our ability becomes to listen with all aspects of our body, decipher the nudges, and respond to the messages. Intuitive awareness is not about measuring our abilities against those of others. It isn't about measuring our abilities past, present, or future. It is about accepting internal life guidance.

Intuitive awareness is a navigational tool that allows us to maneuver through our life lessons and challenges. With intuition as guide, we learn our life lessons and continue to transform into our truest, most authentic self. Embracing our intuitive nature brings us to a place where we transform through self-acceptance. This self-acceptance comes through understanding our intuitive messages and responding to them.

Chapter 12

Shifting to a New Intuitive Reality

Hyperaware, we enter the extraordinary. Intuitive sense facets wide open, the world presents as brighter, louder, more. Until we adjust to this way of perceiving, we are easily distracted and may miss intuitive cues. Anchoring and shielding increase our clarity and minimize opportunities to get stuck in the shenpa of distraction. Staying in this new reality takes courage, curiosity, and daring to wake up to our inner wisdom.

When we practice engaged listening, it is impossible to sleepwalk through life. We may mute the voice of intuition, but it flits around the edges of our consciousness demanding to be heard. It may only be after we unconsciously respond that we realize our intuition was nudging us to action. Recognition of our intuitive response is instrumental to the process of moving along the intuitive awareness continuum.

When aware, all aspects of our being resonate with our intuition. If we miss an intuitive clue, it speaks through another aspect of our being. For example: if we miss an intuitive cue mentally, our body or emotions shout the nudge. If we ignore the message of an intuitive emotion, our body or mind speak to us. As our perception becomes intuitively attuned, we discern the ways intuition speaks through our four aspects: body, mind, spirit, and heart.

When this shift in perception becomes our new reality, our connection to intuition deepens. This deepening does not happen all at once. In fact, we may have moments of weakened connection, but our connection need not stay weak. Through increased intuitive acumen we become more aware of missed messages. Noticing a missed intuitive message means we are strengthening our connection with our inner wisdom.

When we are aware of our connection to inner wisdom, intuition appears everywhere. This is only the beginning. Increasing intuitive awareness requires separating messages from distraction. Anchoring and shielding create a hyperaware filter that filters distractions from our awareness. Distractions filtered, we clearly hear our intuition, decipher, understand, and respond to it.

Tapping into Our Intuition

We gain clarity by tapping into our intuition in a variety of ways: clairvoyance or through seeing, clairaudience or through hearing, clairsentience or through physical sensations , clairalience or through smelling, clairgustance or through tasting, and claircognizance through knowing without knowing why. It doesn't matter which form of clear sensing, we have. What matters is hearing with our intuitive ear and understanding what is said. No matter where we find our self — in the quiet, with a few friends, in a busy social gather, or among strangers, we note how we are impacted. Wherever we find our self, we may need to re-anchor and shield to better grasp the message.

Although we may not be able to hear our intuition, we can name how we are distracted. This practice increases our mindful connection to intuition. First we check our anchor and shield. Then we search for our distractions. Within the space of peace and calm created, we hear the voices of our inner wisdom.

The between is a place of practical patience. When we jump too quickly to a conclusion, we risk hyperextending or negating our intuitive abilities. Hyperextension pulls us from the moment. No longer anchored, the integrity of our shield is compromised. We are overwhelmed by distractions; we miss our intuitive nudges. We suffer intuition fatigue.

Intuition Fatigue and Hyperextension

Intuition fatigue is the result of hyperextension. In this space, everything or nothing appears to be an intuitive message. We waste precious resources on deciphering distractions. We become frustrated at not being able to understand. This spiral is avoided by consciously maintaining an environment of silence. In the silence, we recognize our fatigue, reengage our intuition, and reconnect to the moment to decipher, understand, and integrate the information we receive.

A symptom of hyperextension is believing our illusions are true. No longer guided by our intuition, everything seems to be a message. For example: we overhear someone talking about brake problems on their car and wonder if we need to slow down or speed up in our life. Or, we may believe that this is a sign of our car having brake issues. We believe our intuition is speaking to us; it may not be. Our ability to separate distractions and intuitive cues is limited during hyperextension.

What causes hyperextension? The list is endless, but it may include the following: We are envious of another's capabilities and try to emulate them. Performance anxiety causes us to hyperextend. We might try to access our intuition too broadly moving too quickly along the intuitive awareness continuum.

We need not stay hyperextended. Being mindful is an important step in moving away from hyperextension to hyperawareness. Through contemplative practices, we increase our mindfulness and strengthen our quiet mind. We reduce our angst while increasing our ability to discern the difference between intuition and distraction. Contemplative practice enables us to discover what triggers the hyperextension and move into hyperawareness.

Again, a regular practice of engaged silence and reflection brings clarity. We move from the potential of hyperextension to hyperawareness. Hyperaware, we align to our intuition. The more we practice hyperawareness, the more ways we sense our intuition. We understand that we may not gain an immediate answer; rather, understanding our intuition happens when we need to know.

Synaptic Pruning

Filtering distractions prunes our neural synapses. A benefit of synaptic pruning is increased intuitive resilience. Each time we filter a distraction, we strengthen pathways of intuition while moving away from patterns that catch us in shenpa. We are better able to recognize distractions and not be adversely impacted by them. Think of this as creating your bonsai tree of intuition.

Synaptic pruning creates a pathway on which we live in the three realities simultaneously. Our response flexibility increases. We are less likely to react to distractions; our intuitive awareness strengthens. Please note, intuition is not magic; it is a life skill that is developed through synaptic pruning. We create new pathways of gaining and processing information.

This strengthens our abilities to identify, decipher, understand, and respond to our intuition.

For example: When I have an overwhelming amount of work to accomplish, I anchor into the moment, shield, and listen. As long as I maintain a stance of hyperawareness, my inner voice guides me in the most efficient sequence of task completion. I work much more effectively. Using this skill, I navigate through challenges and learn life lessons.

When we accept our abilities, our view of reality shifts. We open to more accurately seeing. With this shift, our perception is fueled by realistic optimism. We recognize that we possess the abilities necessary to navigate through life. Our confidence grows. We move along the intuitive awareness continuum which further opens us to intuitively seeing.

The gateways into the extraordinary are many. We realize that not everyone has a heightened sense of clairvoyance, the ability to see things intuitively, or clairsentience, the ability to feel things intuitively. I cannot stress this enough — each of us begins with a certain level of intuitive awareness. We each gain intuitive understanding in our own unique way. When we are confident that we are intuitive, our performance anxiety relaxes. As a result, we become aware of intuitive nudges in the ways that work best for us.

Many people that I have met have specific ideas about being intuitive. Often they want a specific way of accessing their intuition or more pronounced ability to access information. Trust that you are exactly where you need to be on the intuitive awareness continuum. What a gift it is to accept that our intuition comes in many shapes and forms that are perfect for us.

When we accept where we are on the continuum and commit to practicing identifying and deciphering our intuition, we are more agile in understanding and responding to our inner wisdom. We are less likely to miss our messages. We recognize that opportunities for increasing our intuitive awareness occur in every moment. Accepting this paradigm shift, we are more resilient, and our response flexibility increases.

Developing a Relationship with Intuition

Believing that we are intuitive is as important as sensing our intuition. This is the precursor to accessing and processing intuitive awareness. While we may never lose concern about intuitively reading something "right," with trust in our abilities we can be daring and courageous in formulating and executing our responses.

We respond to our intuition not because it is safe; rather, we respond in order to live an extraordinary life. With courage, we act upon our nudges, aware of our trepidation. With curious daring, we seek possibilities instead of limitations. We live the life we are meant to live instead of being caught in the fears of what might be.

Acting upon our intuition reminds me of a quote of Thomas Edison's, "I have never failed. I can tell you 10,000 ways not to create a light bulb." Increasing our intuitive awareness happens when we reframe opportunities from failure to growth. When we accept the inevitable — that we misinterpret some intuitive nudges or misidentify some distractions — we strengthen our ability to navigate the triad realities.

Acting with curious daring and courage, we create a space of trust. We recognize that even if our intuition is not validated, this does not mean that the nudge was not accurate or true. It may mean that we have no way of validating it. For example: when I am driving, I may feel that I need to deviate from my planned course. In choosing a different route to the same destination, I trust that my intuition is urging me to change my travel plans for a reason. And, I remember when I did not listen and had a car accident.

Even if we ignore our intuition, the opportunity to act upon it is never lost. It becomes more and more insistent until we must respond. If we do not listen to one intuitive sense facet, others alert us to the presence of intuitive knowing. In fact, the nudge may jump from facet to facet until it grabs our attention.

For example: what begins as a visual cue may re-manifest as a sound or a feeling or an inner knowing. The nudge may manifest any of the four aspects — physical, mental, emotional, or spiritual. When we trust that an intuitive cue is never lost, the pathway to intuition unfolds.

Developing a relationship with intuition requires being comfortable with uncertainty. When we befriend uncertainty instead of expecting life to flow in a particular way, we open to intuitive guidance. Moving consciously and intentionally through the triad realities — the mundane, the between, and the extraordinary — becomes our norm. Eventually we live the three simultaneously.

If an opportunity to explore the intersection of the mundane and extraordinary occurs, we search for the ripples of intuition. This responsive, intentional interaction shifts our perception. Walking amid the realms gives us limitless opportunities to explore how we use our intuitive sense and process information with our intelligences. Our life becomes one of practiced intuitive awareness.

Understanding how we know what we know gives us the power to explore intuitive sense facets not easily accessed. For example: prior to a storm we may notice how our barometric sense facet provides clues to the weather shift. Once we receive this intuitive nudge, we notice how other facets speak to us. We become more agile in our ability to gather information from several intuitive sense facets and use multiple intelligences to process them.

Intuition is more than receiving messages. Intuitive awareness demands that we live in response mode. This movement from reacting to our intuition to discerning a response takes practice. While practice does not make perfect, it does make the connection to our intuition permanent.

Being with a nudge provides the space for us to decipher the message and fashion a more appropriate response. By practicing the 4nons — non-attachment, non-judgment, non-defensiveness, non-violence — we discern if our information is to be used at a later point, if we need to act upon the nudge now, or if we need to be with the nudge while acknowledging uncertainty. There is no standard means of deciphering our intuition.

As we grow in confidence, we may want to share our knowledge with everyone. We may be infected with "expert syndrome." Filled with a desire to use our intuitive knowledge, we may share inappropriate information. Realize that great responsibility comes with being intuitively aware. Live with the belief, "Just because you can, doesn't mean you should."

Ethics and Intuitive Awareness

Intuitive awareness requires that we respond impeccably while recognizing we are fallible and may misinterpret both inner wisdom and distractions. We err on the side of caution. For example: during my time working at a retreat center one of my tasks was to engage volunteers to share Reiki. Even though one volunteer was advised not to share any medically intuitive insights, she did. Her sharing triggered fear in the participant who spoke with me.

I encouraged the woman to see a medical professional if she was concerned. Energetically I could see that there was an imbalance in the energy field of her lower torso. We spoke about how this could have many different causes — mental, emotional, spiritual, or physical. As an intuitive, my intent is to notice and dialogue, not to diagnose. As we conversed, she said that she did have some incontinence issues. She was also ovulating. Those two issues could have been what the Reiki practitioner was noticing.

I do not believe that the Reiki practitioner meant to cause harm. She wanted to share her new-found abilities in ways that would help people. In her desire to help, she crossed an ethical line. Her subjective and objective stances were out of balance. Instead of helping, she caused harm.

This cautionary example reminds us to be mindful during intuitive conversations. Our inner wisdom is a guide and facilitator for our self and others. I believe that a client who poses a question already has the answer. Sharing my vision, I encourage another to engage their wisdom. We are intuitive beings who are meant to share intuition in ways that bring all to a greater understanding.

Just because you can, doesn't mean you should. This is a simple statement of the ethics of intuitive awareness. If you intuitively believe that a friend's spouse is cheating, should you share? Probably not. However, with your intuitive knowing, if the subject arises, you may pose questions that help your friend gain peace while devising a plan of action. That is the compassionate way of intuitive awareness.

Being intuitive is being compassionate. Any information we receive should not be treated lightly. Nor should we share the information without discernment. The journey of increased intuitive awareness requires living the maxim of causing no harm. In doing so, we create the sacred space for our intuition to thrive as we travel the triad realities of mundane, extraordinary, and between.

Chapter 13

Living within the Triad Realities

The key that unlocks our intuition is awareness. Door open, we traverse the extraordinary. In the mundane, we sift through our perceptions to find intuitive messages. Moving from the extraordinary, we enter the between to decipher our intuition and form the response that is shared in the mundane.

With intuitive awareness we identify how illusions inform our reactions. Once identified, our illusions are less likely to define our reality. When we live intuitively, we live authentically. By identifying what distracts us, we gain the power of choice to move from reaction to response. Every time we negate an illusion, our connection to intuition strengthens.

As our connection to intuition strengthens, our permeable boundaries expand. The way we access and process our intuition messages evolves. We connect to our intuitive sense whenever and however possible. Suspending judgment, we trust the information received through our intuition. We reframe our situation into possibilities. Our intuition becomes a life guide.

The Four Aspects of Self

With intuition's guidance we navigate through life finding the Sacred. For me, the Sacred is what I hold in deep reverence; those things in life that are extraordinary and within are most likely to hear the voice of intuition. Discerning what is Sacred to us requires aligning the four aspects of self:

- Beginning with the spirit, we acknowledge how we resonate with the Sacred. Wisdom gained from this aspect increases our ability to name how intuition manifests in the other aspects.

- The heart aspect is home to our emotions. As emotions manifest, we discern to understand our motives, agendas, and assumptions. We identify which emotions are bringers of peace and calm and which are tumultuous, discordant creators of barriers. At peace, we are more likely to clearly recognize and act upon our intuition. A balanced heart aspect increases our ability to recognize the impact of our emotions on our intuition.

- Our mental state stems from our emotional state. When we are emotionally tumultuous, we may not recognize our triggers. We react. The chaos in our mind may result in withdrawal from the world or be a trigger that has us jumping from distraction to distraction. We miss opportunities to recognize the voice of the Sacred. When we are at peace, choosing response is intuitive. Fostering peace within our self strengthens our connection to the Sacred, which in turn increases intuitive awareness.

- We experience three aspects of our being with our physical body. It somatically provides information about our mental and emotional states. Within it, the disharmony or balance of our spirit, heart, and mind manifest. When we are present in our body, we are able to identify what strengthens our connection to inner wisdom and what breaks this fragile connection. Please note, our physical body does not need to be in optimal condition for us to attune to our intuition. Focusing on the many ways our body speaks to us prepares us to hear the voice of inner wisdom speaking through our intuitive sense facets.

Connecting to our intuitive awareness requires accepting our skills and abilities as well as our perceived limitations. Our intuition is a guide, not a bringer of perfection. With intuition, we shift the way we perceive the world. We acknowledge both real and perceived limitations. We gain the potential to dissolve barriers.

These barriers are dissolved when we are at peace. Our four aspects are aligned; we enter a place of clear sight. We perceive and respond to the world through our unique mosaic. That is the goal of intuitive awareness. Realize that if even one aspect is out of balance, we are no longer in optimal alignment with our intuition. To return to intuitive balance, we align each aspect and then bring the four into alignment.

Mindfully Living in Balance

Moving in and out of balance is a lifelong reality. Don't despair if you cannot maintain balance for long periods of time. As our four aspects move in and out of balance, we use mindfulness practices to gain clarity. Practices like sitting meditation, tai chi, yoga, journaling, and walking in nature ground us into the present moment, return us to balance, and strengthen our connection to intuition.

While there is no one formula for enhanced clarity, experimenting with mindfulness practices helps us discover what strengthens our intuitive pathways and prunes our propensity to react. Explore what practices fit best into your journey. As with all things intuitive, experimentation creates authentic, accessible pathways to intuitive knowing.

Remember that our intuitive knowing is accessed only in the present moment. Here we discern what is preventing us from connecting to our intuition. Through the power of choice, we bring our body, mind, spirit, and heart into balance, or we choose the illusion that the knowledge of the imbalance is enough. The former choice brings us into alignment with our intuition; the latter weakens our connection to it.

Each time we realign, the resulting balance strengthens our unique mosaic. As we practice accessing our intuition from this mosaic, it becomes easier to bring our self back into alignment and deepen our connection to each of the triad realities. Through this connection we more easily identify and process our inner wisdom.

Even when we are not in alignment, our intuition runs on a continuous loop. Unless we have created calm at our core, we miss the majority of information the first time it cycles through. This intuitive information is seldom lost. Eventually the intuitive message gains volume and becomes too loud to ignore. We need not wait that long. Realignment strengthens the voice of our internal guidance.

Maintaining a thriving internal calm clears the way to our intuition and allows us to stop subtle imbalances from being barriers to our intuition. One way to lessen a barrier is to listen to both intuition and distractions in each aspect. This does not need to be a time-consuming activity. Per Jill Bolte Taylor, it takes an emotion 90 seconds to move through and out of the physical body. Using this 90-second life span of emotion as a model, we can do a 90-second check-in to listen to what each of our aspects tell us.

For example: if we are anxious about an upcoming event, our mind may not stop replaying the same monologue loop. We may find it difficult to sit quietly. With practice, the imbalance behind our agitation can be quickly identified in 90 seconds or less. We name how our distractions hijack us. We anchor and shield. We regain balance. We go beyond our distractions to listen to our intuition.

Unless we acknowledge the ebb and flow of balance and imbalance in our aspects, we risk becoming overwhelmed with intuition fatigue. Remember that in a state of intuition fatigue, everything or nothing appears to be an intuitive message. Not anchored in the moment, our shield no longer protects us from the bombardment of information. Everything or nothing seems like an intuitive message.

We minimize fatigue by knowing our triggers. We begin by recognizing that distractions are not the only things that unbalance us. Intuitive cues may do so as well. Our inner wisdom speaks to us through the cracks of our misalignment. These cues alert us to the symptoms of the imbalance and its root cause.

Strengthening Our Connection to Intuition

Being intuitive means seeing nothing in our life as negative. For example: I have found that in times of high emotion, such as grief, or in times of great stress, like unemployment, my ability to notice intuitive messages intensifies. Instead of being overwhelmed, I objectively gather information. My powers of discernment increase; I filter the distractions from inner knowing.

We increase our inner calm through practice. For example: if we are more likely to process our intuition intrapersonally, we practice accessing it when we are alone. We create a quiet space with a minimum of distractions. Try this: to bolster your intrapersonal intuitive processor, find ways to use your solitary time to practice identifying, deciphering, understanding, and responding to your inner wisdom.

If we are more likely to be aware of our intuition interpersonally, we practice in places where people are. We consciously connect with others by talking to others including strangers. We people watch or surround ourselves with community. Although we do not fish for information, we are alert to information as it comes our way. (By fishing, I mean that we intentionally and uninvited enter the energy of another person to gain intuitive information.)

The same is true of the other intuitive processors. By experimenting with our intelligences, we discover how we process our intuition and naturally increase our intuitive awareness. We grow adept in combining processors to interpret intuitive messages. Through each sense facet and our intuitive processors, we enhance our ability to access intuitive information whether it is manifesting internally or externally.

By trusting our abilities, we may notice additional challenges with which to refine our abilities. (A challenge is an exaggerated opportunity to access and use your intuition.) As our skills and abilities increase, our intuitive awareness grows. As our intuitive understanding expands, we discover new ways we receive information and are given opportunities to use additional intuitive sense processors.

For example: It is easier for me to listen to my intuition with little or no outside stimuli. Being alone helps me focus on the nudges. But in order to stretch my abilities, I practice in less private, more social environments. As a result, my intuitive interactions with clients no longer require additional prep time. I open to the message and expect to discern it.

Regularly connecting to your intuition is important. Begin each morning by setting and refining intuitive space. Throughout the day, no matter where you find yourself, reset your connection to your intuition. Set intent, ground, shield, and focus. Even brief moments of reconnection have the power to move you into a place of greater awareness.

Shielding and anchoring are vital to intuitive space. A shield encompasses the physical area you find yourself in and acts as an early warning system. There are no rules about where and how you create this space. An intuitive extends internal calm into the external environment — even the clothes and jewelry we wear contribute to its stability. The intent of the shield is to increase awareness so that any nudge is amplified, and our attention is drawn to it.

The creation of intuitive space may involve ritual. I set my intent each morning and evening using the seven directions. The seven directions are north, south, east, west, earth, sky, and self. Is there anything magical about these directions? No, but when I use these seven directions to set my intuitive calm, my connection to intuition is stronger.

Intuitive calm may also be created by objects: a candle, images, a sculpture, a chair, a meditation cushion, a blanket. We may designate a specific place in our home and/or prepare a kit to carry with us. We may use specific rituals when engaging in certain activities. For me, when I write intuitively, I use a specific pen and notebook.

How we create our intuitive calm is unique to each of us. Our intent is to align our essence with the vibration of our intuition. There is no wrong way to do this. There is only your way. The way you set calm and connect to your intuition will shift over time or change, depending upon your circumstances.

Through enhanced intuitive awareness, we create calm that permeates every moment. In order to strengthen our access point to intuition, practice is required. Practice upon waking and at the end of each day helps focus our attention on the voices of our intuition. These two anchor points create a bridge on which our inner wisdom flows. Each time we renew our connection to our intuitive calm, the bridge strengthens.

Creating a calm where our intuition thrives becomes as natural as our connection to intuition. There is no science and no formula to creating internal and external intuitive calm. We listen to our inner wisdom and sustain our connection to it. We explore how to transform the way we live both internally and externally. We increase our clarity. The greater the clarity, the better we focus our awareness in ways that bring understanding to our intuition as we navigate the triad realities.

Chapter 14

The Intuitive Cipher

Hyperaware, we access our intuition 24/7. While some of our inner knowing can be literal, most messages are shrouded in metaphor and symbol. To make sense of our intuition, we decipher it using our intelligences. By accessing and processing our intuition, each of us creates a unique cipher or set of tools used to understand our intuitive messages.

The beginning of cipher creation is the identification and deciphering of cues. For example: when I practice accessing my intuition, I focus my attention on the extraordinary without attempting to define what I am sensing. Being hyperaware without judging or defending is foundational to interpreting the message. Remember, holding tightly to our preconceived interpretation makes it difficult to use full-body listening as a deciphering tool.

The Four Aspects as Cipher Tools

The four aspects of our self — mind, spirit, body, and heart — are integral to building our cipher. Through each our intuition speaks. Information impacts our body aspect through physical sensations. An intuitive message manifests in the mental aspect as an image or words. Within the heart aspect, our emotions speak. Spiritually we feel the presence of another being or sense messages.

Using information gained from the four aspects, we decode our intuitive messages using tools. These tools vary depending upon the intuitive and the situation. One tool is dream interpretation. Dreams carry powerful intuitive messages for us. Try this: write down everything you remember about a dream. Include any additional impressions you gain as you write. If your intuition speaks to you during this practice, write down what your intuition surfaces. Research any symbols you do not understand. This is part of the process of deciphering.

For example: during a dream I found myself in a flooded basement with my sister. There were three snakes swimming toward us. My sister pushed me into the snakes. They bit me. I was rushed to the hospital. Swollen with toxins, I was in great pain. Eventually, the poisons left my body. When I was released from the hospital, I asked my sister why she pushed me into the snakes. She said, "You were the only one who could transmute the poison."

Through interpreting this dream, I was better able to understand the life lessons gifted to me through my family of origin. I understood my role in my family was to transmute energetic toxins for my family. But, the interpretation did not stop there. Later, I was able to discern an additional message of the dream. The snake is an ancient healing symbol. The dream was an affirmation of my study of natural health. This dream verified how healing was woven into my soul purpose.

The Intuitive Awareness Continuum

As we move along the intuitive awareness continuum, we start where we are. We respond to intuition as it manifests. It might be in a dream, the words of another, a part of nature. When we are hyperaware, our intuition speaks to us at any given moment from seemingly unlikely sources. As we interpret and respond to the message, we gain clarity in that moment. We may receive additional understanding as we grow into the intuitive message as I did with the dream of the snake.

No matter where we find our self on the intuitive awareness continuum, we never censor what we receive. Censoring is a distraction. Instead of censoring, we use our filters to recognize what distracts us. We are aware that each cue is providing information even if we are unable to clearly see. As we gain experience and confidence, our abilities to decipher the messages increase.

As we filter information, we identify and attend to intuitive nudges. We notice how our intuitive sense facets pair with our processors. Although the same facets do not always pair with the same processors, being mindful of how they interface increases our ability to access our intuition. This pairing is important for our cipher. As we gain a greater understanding of how we receive and process intuition, we increase our ability to identify, understand, and respond to intuitive messages.

As a cipher element, each intelligence or intuitive processor grows stronger when we intentionally use it. For example: over the last decade my ability to process intuitive cues with my naturalistic intelligence has strengthened. By spending time in nature, I more easily identify and then discern the messages inherent in animals, plants, and the weather. While I may not immediately interpret their meanings, I do recognize the symbols.

A Strengthener of Deciphering: Meditatio/Oratio/Contemplatio

For me, the three-fold way of meditatio/oratio/contemplatio strengthened my deciphering abilities. Let's use this as a ciphering tool example In an environment of meditatio, we focus on the extraordinary, identify intuitive messages, and forge intuitive pathways. Our attention is naturally drawn to intuition's voice. This is not the only purpose of meditatio. Through it, we identify how we receive and process our inner wisdom. It provides greater understanding of intuition as a guide for the whole of our life. With meditatio, we formulate our oratio or intent to understand.

Oratio is the petition of our intent. It is based upon both our awareness that we are intuitive and our intent to understand and apply intuition in our life. Through the practice of oratio, we strengthen our mindful stance. Our oratio is forged through the interaction of our internal monologue and external stimuli. With awareness, we understand the power of intuition to guide us even when we are not consciously aware. Conscious intent roots us into the present moment. Intent, both conscious and unconscious, forms the bridge between our meditatio and contemplatio.

When we enter contemplatio, we suspend our judgments, assumptions, and defenses while opening to whatever our intuition shares. We accept that any personal or cultural meanings may be barriers to understanding. During contemplatio, we listen open to the intuitive meaning.

Free Association as a Ciphering Tool

Listening while engaging in free association provides additional cues. For example: from soda to cheese curls to oranges to carrots to peppers to sherbet — at one point, most of what I ate was the color orange. At the same time, I realized that I had an aversion to wearing the color orange. So, using these two pieces of information, which on the surface appear contradictory, I use the process of meditatio/oratio/contemplatio.

The color orange is related to the sacral chakra. Through this energy center we give birth to all of our creations. The color orange represents enthusiasm, creativity, and stimulation. I am ingesting the color that leads me to believe I need to provide sustenance for my creative process. I don't like to wear the color orange. I understood the message to tell me that I am preventing the manifestation of my creativity. My interpretation: I want to create, am feeding my creativity, but am being stopped by fear.

Now comes the power of choice. Will I allow my intuition to nudge me into finding ways to recognize the fear and move through it? Or, will I allow the trepidation to overwhelm any creative urges? In order to respond to this intuition, I notice any time I am drawn to eating orange foods or acting on my aversion to wearing the color orange.

I actively find ways to embrace my creative self. I may write, make jewelry, or paint. I commit to a weekly blog post and begin another draft of my book. I creatively concoct a meal. Identifying my block is an opportunity to name my fear and consciously engage in activities that unlock my creativity.

In this example, a color and foods were metaphors. Although we do receive literal messages, often our nudges are symbols that must be deciphered. Gathering information about symbols and metaphors is critical to building a cipher based upon experience and intuitive responses.

When I consciously began my journey with intuition, I accumulated a variety of books on nature symbols, animal totems, the meaning of colors, dream interpretation, and other subjects. I have studied religious traditions for over 40 years to better understand rituals, sacred symbols, and the role of prophets. Now much of this information can be accessed through the internet.

No matter how you choose to access information and build your cipher, the wider your knowledge base, the easier it is to decipher intuitive messages. You don't have to memorize the meaning of everything; you just need to be able to discern potential interpretations and decide for yourself the meaning of the message.

Origin of Intuitive Cues

Our intuitive cues exist in many forms from literally understood to esoteric and symbolic. Examples of a literal intuitive cue: we may be urged to take surface roads instead of highways. We may be unable to get the thought of someone out of our head until we contact them. Esoteric and symbolic intuitive nudges may require research. For example: we may see a flock of birds and need to ascertain the meaning of it in order to decipher the message. We may feel aversion regarding a color and study the meaning of that color to know the intuitive message.

As I build my intuitive cipher, so does my confidence and ability to interpret, understand, and respond to my intuitive messages. At times, I am amazed when my words and actions are exactly what is needed in the moment. This intuitive synchronization shows me that there are no hard rules about deciphering intuition. We may come to an instantaneous understanding or it might take us longer to unravel the meaning. We use the process of meditatio/oratio/contemplatio both consciously and unconsciously as we discern the message.

It may only be after our response that we realize that intuition guided us to act as we did. For example: when I am working on a project, I may wonder about a deadline only to receive a text message with the answer. When we are open, intuition's silent internal voice communicates to us. This wordless communication, intuitive communion, occurs when you finish a close friend's sentence or pose a question before someone utters it.

As we decipher intuitive messages, we become increasingly hyperaware of the subtleties of the message. No longer believing in coincidence, we see synchronicity in our life. This is not fatalism. Through synchronicity we shift from a reactionary life to one of response. With intuitive awareness, we listen to life messages and meet our challenges.

For example: I once dated a man who, after about a year, shared his discomfort about how I communicated. I often asked him specific questions about things I did not know had occurred. My intuition led me to ask questions that had no tangible basis. He attempted, but was unable, to hide certain actions that were detrimental to the relationship. My spontaneous inner knowing made him uncomfortable; the relationship did not survive. But, I discovered that relying on my intuition aligns me with what really is.

Through this experience, I was reminded about the importance of consciously connecting to intuition. Being mindful during each interaction leads to an understanding of how intuition is informing our responses and how distractions are at the root of our reactions. We notice how intuition is guiding us. We respond using our intuition.

Full-Body Listening as a Ciphering Tool

Full-body listening is a primary skill in our cipher box. Through it, we identify more subtle nuances of inner wisdom. Bi-listening is an aspect of full-body listening. We listen to what is occurring internally or in all aspects of our being while attending to the external world. Unless we are fully present, this is an almost impossible task. Backward focused or forward focused, we miss intuitive nudges. We are too busy focusing on fears, regrets, and worries to hear what our intuition shares.

Even when we are in a state of hyperawareness, we may still miss all or a portion of our intuitive whispers. We do not let this deter us. Being in the moment is the only place to hear our intuition. We realize that an important intuitive knowing surfaces again and again until we get it. It continues speaking to us until we hear and understand. Those intuitive knowings provide some of the greatest tools in our cipher.

Remember intuitive information is layered and multifaceted. If we miss one intuitive nudge, it reappears through another intuitive sense facet. If we still do not catch it, the nudge appears in other facets until we are able to see it. I have often said that when I ignore or miss my intuitive nudges, they shout at me until I have no alternative but to listen. This shouting appears in ways that the most aligned intelligence can process. To build our cipher, we pay attention to those intuitive shouts.

Recognizing that an intuitive whisper is never lost reduces our performance anxiety. So does the realization that cues from different intuitive sense facets are deciphered by using different intelligences. Intuition finds the holes in our defenses. It seeps into our conscious mind in ways that grab our attention. Once we decipher it, we might reflect if, and when, the nudge manifested before. This practice helps us discover how intuitive messages present and is another aspect of our cipher.

Our growing skills assist us in recognizing our intuitive nudges. I might consciously focus on something in my environment and notice how it triggers intuitive knowing. For example: I meditate upon the artwork of Susan Seddon Boulet. Her paintings are an extraordinary blend of humans, animals, and nature. Reflecting on the images often reveals intuitive messages.

Listening to music strengthens the pathway of inner knowing. Connecting to our aural intelligence, we move to a rhythm and discover a nudge within the lyrics. Or, in the movement of our bodies we may kinesthetically dislodge a piece of somatic intuitive awareness. Since we are electromagnetic, a sound resonates throughout our being, bringing the four aspects of self into greater alignment releasing inner knowing.

Still other external tools may be spiritual or metaphysical. Incense may trigger olfactory intuition. The use of tarot cards may provide additional insight. A pendulum may increase our awareness of disruptions in our energy body or the energy bodies of others. Meditation, prayer beads, or other contemplative tools connect our body/mind/spirit/heart. This connection creates a pathway for intuitive flow.

Moving along the intuitive awareness continuum means using both internal and external tools. We may use tools like writing or cooking that, on the surface, do not seem to be intuitive enhancing. These activities engage multiple intelligences that together bring forth understanding. As we move along the intuitive awareness continuum, we experiment, play, and just enjoy the unfolding of our intuitive connection. We are not complacent in our abilities. As an intuitive our desire is to grow a cipher that mirrors where we are on the intuitive awareness continuum.

Our journey with ciphering is not magical; the purpose is to understand how we connect with awareness. As we begin to filter our intuition, we discover that some intuitive messages are more accessible than others. As we explore the many ways our intuition manifests, we become more adept in discerning both overt and subtle inner wisdom. Moving along the intuitive awareness continuum, we recognize other ways that our intuition speaks.

To build our cipher, we start where we are by exploring the more easily accessible pathways of intuition. Moving along our intuitive awareness continuum, we gain a greater understanding of how intuition manifests. We actively seek intuitive cues through less used intuitive sense facets. By processing the information in these previously unexplored facets, we become increasingly more intuitive aware.

Chapter 15

Within the Intuitive Sense Facets

There is nothing magical about our intuitive sense. By now, I hope you understand that. Our intuitive sense, rooted in our core, is our life guide, our internal GPS. We activate it by cultivating our quiet mind. Within this space of clarity, we sense what is broadcast through our intuitive sense facets and process the information using our intelligences.

Although we may recognize the voice of intuition in any moment, through conscious alignment of our four aspects, we intentionally listen to our inner wisdom. With the information gathered, we decipher messages. We gain insights into our challenges and life lessons. Our intuitive messages are not magical; rather these messages provide a blueprint for a more balanced life. I call this a life filled with sacred calm.

Sacred Calm

Sacred calm is safe calm. We create sacred calm through our connection to the extraordinary. This connection reflects our authentic self. Peering into the reflection, we identify obstacles in our path. Acting with courage and curious daring, we break the paralysis of fear. Within the sacred calm, we grow our hyperawareness and navigate the path of inner knowing.

Through our sacred calm we traverse the triad realities: the mundane, the extraordinary, and the between. With hyperawareness, we sense these three realities individually and collectively. We notice the many ways our intuitive sense speaks to us. We gain clarity by tapping into:

- clairvoyance: Through the intuition of sight, we are drawn to certain physical elements or notice things not physically present. We see the tangible and intangible messages.

- clairaudience: We hear with clarity the words of another, a song, our internal monologue. These messages manifest through many sense facets.

- clairsentience: Physical sensations provide information necessary for us to formulate responses in the world. We intuitively validate any sensations we have in our body.

- clairalience: Intuition draws our attention to tangible and intangible odors that provide intuitive cues.

- clairgustance: We gain intuitive cues through our sense of taste.

- claircognizance: We have an intuitive knowing without knowing why.

Through the six "clairs" we connect to our sacred calm. Within this space, we recognize the voice of intuition. One way of setting this sacred calm is through our breath. With each inhale, we breathe in the energy of creation. We acknowledge ruah, the breath behind the breath that Andy Caponigro writes about in In the Miracle of the Breath. Through the conscious inhale of ruah, we affirm that the Sacred is part of us. By focusing on ruah, we are claircognizant of the weave of the triad realities — extraordinary, mundane, and between.

We ride on the wings of ruah, inhaling to consciously decipher intuitive cues, understand messages, and form responses. On our exhale we respond to intuition. With each breath, we continue the cycle of accessing, processing, and responding to our intuition. Through this cycle, barriers to our intuition crumble as we bring our body, mind, spirit, and heart into alignment.

The more we align with our inner wisdom, the easier it becomes to live each moment being guided by intuition. Intuitive awareness is no longer an isolated event. We move into neural synchrony with others. It is this connection of neural pathways of two people that increases our ability to communicate with one another and collectively. Through this heart-to-heart, soul-to-soul connection we, as intuitives, interact.

Neural Synchrony

What is neural synchrony? It is a deep connection between two people that taps into all from aspects of our being. Neural synchrony is a connection between two people through which intuition flows. How does neural synchrony work? We may complete another's sentence or answer a question before it is asked. We may feel the need to contact someone and act upon it.

When we connect through neural synchrony, our perspective shifts. We open to what connects us. We identify what builds and sustains barriers. Although it primarily serves to increase connection and understanding between people, this synchrony boosts our intuitive awareness. Through it, we can intuitively analyze how we receive information from our intuitive sense facets and our four aspects. Neural synchrony can bring us to sacred calm. It may also shatter that calm when we are unaware.

Once the sacred calm is developed, we never stop practicing with and strengthening our connection to our four aspects, intuitive sense facets, and our intelligences. We notice which facets are more balanced and which are currently inaccessible. We discern which intelligences are used for processing. With this information we stretch our intuitive awareness.

Within the sacred calm, we discern when to process our intuition. We gather information knowing that we may not have time to analyze our intuition stream in that moment. If we do not have time to decipher, we wait until we do. When we are able, we move into a hyper-aware state and engage in meditatio/oratio/contemplatio to identify and process the cues. Understanding is possible when we discern the message objectively.

Practice Makes Permanent

Each time we practice listening to intuition from a specific intuitive sense facet, that facet becomes easier to access. Practice may not make perfect, but it does create a permanent connection to our intuitive awareness. As we become more proficient in identifying the messages from the primary facets, our awareness of the origin of intuition's voice increases.

As we develop our skills and abilities, we experience the nuances of intuition that come from our connection to secondary sense facets. For example: we may hear words with our physical ears while accessing additional information through our mind's ear. This inner hearing may manifest as actual words or even images. We may hear the words of another as clearly as if they are spoken. We may also hear the message embedded, unspoken words, within what another says without tangible evidence.

Our intuition also serves as a truth detector. I have found that when someone is not truthful that I have a flat or a heavy sensation in my mouth. This information is relayed through the ionic facet. When you are claircognizant, ask yourself what intuitive sense facets triggered this knowing.

Intuitive aromas nudge us into awareness. Each provides messages for us to decipher. A message is only the starting point. Because it is easy for our sense of smell to become desensitized, we may subconsciously receive a cue, react to it, and have no idea why we reacted. In those moments, entering the sacred calm to engage in full-body listening may provide the answer. We gain information unconsciously through our vomeronasal facet.

Touch provides the greatest cluster of secondary facets. We touch with our hands. We feel textures, heat, and moisture. We may use our geogravimetric sense facet to discern mass differences or sense a change in pressure using the barometric sense facet. Of course, we feel pain by touching.

Intuitively we use our sense of touch without physically touching another. Holding our hands several inches above the body, we may notice a tingling in our palms, an invisible barrier, or some other sensation. When this happens, we have connected to another's energy body. Entering neural synchrony with another, we gain information. Through this energetic resonance we are better able to understand the messages of the secondary facets.

Increasing Intuitive Awareness

The key to increasing our intuitive awareness is not about knowing where to look for intuition. Increased awareness comes from knowing how to look. When we know how to shift our perception to enter the sacred calm, we naturally focus on our intuitive message. This shift in perception requires consciously looking beyond the mundane. With a change in perception, we boost our ability to access our intuitive sense facets.

When we access information through our nineteen intuitive sense facets, distractions separate from inner knowing. We can increase our intuitive awareness by exploration and experimentation. This involves consciously accessing information through different facets. We begin with those intuitive sense facets that we access more easily and then challenge our self by practicing with others.

Inner wisdom is a constant stream that enters our consciousness through our intuitive sense. The more often we connect with each facet, the easier it is to sense our intuition speaking. As we move along the intuitive awareness continuum, we continue to engage in listening with all our sense facets.

Exploring within the Sacred Calm

Within sacred calm we explore our intelligences to better understand how we process our intuition. We use similar techniques and skills used to practice accessing intuition to process our intuition with our intelligences. We practice connecting the facets to specific intelligences for processing. For example: We may hear an intuitive message and then walk (kinesthetic intelligence) to decipher it.

Through intentionally resting in sacred calm, we gain new opportunities to further explore the connections between our intuitive nudges and the ways we process them. In a controlled environment of sacred calm, we create conditions to process, using each of our intelligences separately.

During these times of experimentation, we notice how each intuitive processor either increases our awareness or blocks deciphering. We recognize our better ways of obtaining and processing information from the most inaccessible facets and intelligences. With practice, these "better ways" shift to include additional facets and intelligences.

No matter which intelligences are more easily accessed, we use all our intelligences, to some degree, to process our intuition. Although we are more likely to trust the message revealed from more easily accessed intelligences, reflection and introspection are means to better understand how we access and process our intuitive awareness.

Our goal is to understand how we process our intuition and, in doing so, strengthen our connections to our inner wisdom. Sacred calm is a playground for us to explore our inner wisdom by moving from mundane to extraordinary to between dynamically. With increased fluidity, we intuitively notice more and become intuitively adept.

Our life is a laboratory of intuitive discovery. Through intuitive awareness, we better understand how fear fuels our reactions and what is at the root of our responses. We clearly see that our responses connect us to our authentic self; our reactions mire us in illusion. When we intuitively nurture what is true, we respond in ways that diminish the effects of our illusions and strengthen our connection to our true self.

Accessing our intuition does not make us better, smarter, or special. Intuition is a life tool. Through our intuitive awareness we navigate our life path. Challenges become opportunities for transformation. We recognize that intuition is and always has been our constant companion and lifelong guide.

When I am conscious of the many ways the voice of my intuition speaks, I recognize how I often respond to intuition unconsciously. I am humbled by my unconscious ability to listen and respond to my intuitive whispers. No matter how I access my intuition, it empowers me. Through it, I am better able to be present in the moment. When I listen with intuitive awareness, I make life altering decisions that lead to transformation.

Moving along the intuitive awareness continuum is a lifelong journey. When we consciously agree to deepen our connection to our intuitive nature, the transition points connecting the extraordinary, mundane, and between become porous. We move amid the triad realities simultaneously as we decipher information and formulate responses. We live as a holistic intuitive being.

As an intuitive, we recognize that we are a mosaic comprised of our intuitive sense, four aspects of self, and our intuitive processors. This mosaic is continually refined within our sacred calm. Through our mosaic, we live in ways that continue to propel us from the mundane into the extraordinary and through the between only to return to the mundane with an intuitive response.

Chapter 16

Into the Sacred Mosaic

At the conception of our spirit, the Creator carves off a piece of Itself. Blowing this ember into us, our sacred spark or spirit is awakened. From the conception of our spirit, this divine spark powers our body, mind, and heart. While our physical vessel is the visible receptacle for the other three aspects, it is not the most important aspect. It is the framework on which the mosaic of our mind, spirit, and heart evolve.

Components of Our Sacred Mosaic

When we accept that we are a mosaic of four aspects — body/mind/ spirit/heart — our paradigm shifts. Within this new paradigm, our intuitive essence manifests. As we open our self to intuitive messages, opportunities for personal evolution present. We live consciously aligning the four aspects of self. Although the four aspects need not be in alignment to hear the voice of our intuition, when the they collaborate, we are hyperaware of our intuition.

Our divine spark lights the path to our intuition. We realize that we cannot have a spiritual life independent of our physical existence nor can we divorce our thoughts from our emotions. We understand that we cannot separate any aspect from the whole or elevate one aspect above another. To do so is to silence the voice of our intuition.

Our physical aspect is the receptacle for the other aspects. It is a partner, not a servant. As a sentry, its reactions serve as an early warning system. The other three aspects trigger sensations within the sentry. For example: we may feel a sudden pain coupled with an "aha" moment. We acknowledge the sensation and discern if it is intuitive or distractive.

Our body is not the only aspect that provides clues about distractions and intuition. In order to discover how our emotional body is out of alignment, we attend to both our body and our mind — we listen to our internal monologue and how our body reacts to it. We question if emotional reactions are distractions or intuitive messages. We name how we get hooked by distractions and react.

Connecting to our divine spark, we live in intuitive response. This response is the result of a flexible, open heart. Our emotions are the energy of our heart aspect. When they are disheveled, our connection to intuition is frayed. A balanced heart aspect is key to identifying, deciphering, and responding with our intuitive awareness. Heart aligned, we are less likely to be led by our emotions; rather, our emotions become emissaries of our intuition.

Our mind is seldom quiet. At any given point, it is filled with a barrage of thoughts fueled by our beliefs, judgments, and assumptions. Try this: set a timer for 90 seconds and listen to what your mind is saying. Notice where your thoughts draw you. Ask, how am I drawn from the moment? What distracts me? What centers me? In this non-present space, distraction-fueled illusions overwhelm us.

Mind misaligned, the flow of our intuition is reduced to intermittent sparks of knowing that are seemingly impossible to connect with. By attending to our internal monologue, we filter through illusions freeing our self from distractions. No longer tangled with distractions bred from our thoughts, our mind realigns with the other aspects. The connection to our intuition clears.

Our spiritual aspect interfaces with the extraordinary. This connection is strengthened by contemplative practice. Through mindfulness our spirit twines with our body, mind, and heart. We become a balanced whole, a beacon for our inner wisdom. A sound body, attentive mind, and open heart connected to an actualized spirit is the foundation of our objectivity.

Living Imperfectly, Living Intuitively

No aspect is more important than the others. When we attend to all aspects — body, mind, spirit, and heart, we create the pathway of alignment. With the four aspects balanced, we are optimal, open, effective conduits. But, we will not remain that way. It is inevitable that we move in and out of balance. While we may never be 100 percent balanced, 100 percent of the time, we can minimize the time we spend unaligned.

By accepting that we are imperfect, our performance anxiety decreases. We do not have to get everything right every time. With this acceptance, we open further to intuition. As our inner wisdom wafts through the cracks of our imperfections, we open to the truth instead of measuring, labeling, or comparing. We notice imbalances and use our intuition to bring harmony to our four aspects.

As we identify, decipher, and respond to inner knowing, our approach to life shifts. Instead of being unaware in the mundane, we sense the extraordinary inherent in each moment. We actively seek the extraordinary by accessing cues internally and externally. We realize that life, even in the darkest moments, is filled with possibilities. We intuitively evaluate those possibilities. We live our life fully awake, alert, and alive. Our mosaic evolves within connected triad realities: mundane, extraordinary, between.

Hyperaware, we wake to challenges. The way we see our interactions shift. Instead of feeling victimized, we see our life as a sequence of opportunities for growth. While we may be unable to stop life's harshness from impacting us, each moment of awareness provides opportunities to dig into the fertile ground of our being unearthing our intuitive knowing.

We may not be able to consistently maintain a state of hyperawareness, but to a certain degree, we are always awake, alert, and alive. In those moments, we recognize both challenges and distractions manifesting in each moment. We build upon these moments to more rapidly identify our challenges and meet them more quickly.

Although intuition continually resonates within our mosaic, we are not guaranteed any level of intuitive expertise or ability. We are guaranteed ongoing opportunities to evolve our abilities. When we nurture our intuition, we strengthen our ability to connect with it. As we grow our intuitive awareness, we continue to assess imbalances of our four aspects and use the knowledge gained to realign the aspects individually and collectively.

When all four aspects are in harmony, our ability to recognize, identify, understand, and respond is enhanced. If our aspects are out of balance — one individually or several together — it is more difficult, but not impossible, to hear our intuition. With practice, we notice when our inner voice speaks, name any imbalances, and respond regardless of aspect alignment. Remember, practice makes permanent our connection to intuition.

Our mosaic, as with our journey with intuition, is not static. Within sacred calm, we evolve this mosaic. A calm fostered clarity grows holistically in all four aspects of our being. Within this holistic growth, our quiet mind awakens. It speaks. We listen. We are able to sustain hyperawareness for greater periods of time and access our intuition revealed in our body, mind, spirit, and heart.

In order to amplify the message received in one aspect, we focus on other aspects. For example: we may become anxious. To determine if it is a distraction or an intuitive cue, we listen to our internal monologue by checking the emotions pulsing from our body. We listen to how our body is impacted. Next, we check in to both our mind and spirit aspects. Gaining a holistic image of how we are impacted, we separate distraction from intuition. We then decipher the message.

The Pause

We rest in sacred calm without scheduled activity as we quietly notice what draws our attention. We engage in mindful activities in order to rest within the pause. What is the pause? Perhaps it is better to begin with what it is not. Rhythm is found not in musical notes but in the spaces between them. Meaning is found not in the words but in the silence between syllables. Understanding of Tai Chi body/mind/spirit connection is not found in the inhale/exhale but in the space between them. The pause is found in every thing we do. Through the pause our intuitive awareness activates. We notice nuances, even patterns, and find meaning within them. Those pauses are the weave that connects the essence of who we are to our intent and action.

Perhaps one of our greatest challenges is learning to live in the pause. We can only be in that space when we are in the moment. The past no longer pulls us at with its regrets and remorse. The future's lure of hopes and dreams loses its allure. Through the pause, We focus our awareness on the present moment. We better access our intuition in times of distraction.

Of course, when we quiet the physical world around us, the volume of our internal monologue is raised. All of our thoughts and emotions are amplified until we cannot ignore them. To cultivate sacred calm, we listen to our internal monologue while practicing the 4nons — non-attachment, non-judgment, non-defensivenss, and non-violence. We are aware that judgments, assumptions, and beliefs are distractions that fuel the many illusions we accept.

We accept that at the root of both tumult and peace are emotions. Sacred calm requires an acknowledgement of any turmoil present. Try this: acknowledge an emotion. Sit with the emotion for 90-seconds while practicing the 4nons. This helps us to let go of the force of the emotion and to return to intuitive equilibrium. Note: you may have to practice this 90-second pause several times to get optimal results.

Next, notice how emotions impact thoughts and how they subtly and overtly trigger reactions. Through sacred calm, be aware of how the heart aspect imbalances the whole or brings it closer to harmony. Through emotions, recognize when the mosaic is not optimally primed to recognize and process inner wisdom. This learning is an important part of your intuitive cipher.

The fourth aspect of our sacred mosaic is spirit. Our spirit is comprised of energetic strands that weave through all aspects bringing them into collaborative alignment. Engaging in contemplative practices strengthens the whole spiritual weave. Through mindfulness, we feed the sacred calm of our spirit. Sacred calm then travels to the other aspects, igniting awareness in the whole of our life.

Through self-awareness, we identify the cracks of our mosaic caused by distractions and the unsuccessful meeting of life challenges. Instead of despairing at our state of disrepair, we see any cracks as opportunity. Through information gained intuitively, we fill the cracks and return to whole. Listening and responding to our intuition, we move into greater harmony.

Spiritual Kintsugi

We can heal our self by returning to wholeness through the practice of the spiritual kintsugi. What is spiritual kintsugi? We've defined spirit. Let's now define kintsugi. Let's begin with Raku pottery. This Japanese pottery is valued for more than its original beauty. In fact, when a piece of raku is cracked or broken, it is seldom thrown away. Instead, the pottery is repaired by pouring gold into the cracks. This process is called "kintsugi." Although its beauty is altered, the repaired pottery is stronger than the original piece.

I have read stories about people breaking their pottery so that it could be repaired — the cracks filled with gold. To some, a repaired pot with gold lines streaking through it is more beautiful than the original. So it is with our self. When we heal our self, we are not who we were before. Our authentic self is reflected in the beauty of our transformed mosaic.

Healing means a return to wholeness, not a restoration to the original form. Within this wholeness, our body, mind, spirit, and heart align. We move along the intuitive awareness continuum. The beauty of our sacred spark shines from our thoughts, words, and actions. Our intuition sings forth a new melody. We decipher and respond to our inner knowing.

Why is the process of spiritual kintsugi so important? Without breaking our vessel, motes of intuition would not have escaped into our awareness. Much like the shouting of intuition, the cracks in any aspect of our mosaic capture our attention. It presents the opportunity to engage our sacred calm. Within it we gain the clarity to decipher and understand intuitive whispers. In determining the message, we repair our mosaic.

In sacred calm, we connect to all four aspects of our being. Integrating intuitive messages into our life is the process of spiritual kintsugi. As an intuitive, we view all responses to our intuition as healing. Each repairs our mosaic. With healing we are stronger than before and better able to take on new challenges as the gold of the sacred flow through our veins.

Spiritual kintsugi connects us to our quiet mind, the power behind the weaving of the spirit with other aspects. While the spirit is the energizer, the quiet mind is the unifier of our mosaic. It is activated during full-body listening. With full-body listening, we attend to the sensations of our body, the thoughts in our mind, and the reactions of our emotion. We discern what each tells us intuitively.

Clearing Distractions

When we cultivate an atmosphere of sacred calm and practice engaged silence, we are better able to clear the clutter of distractions. This clearing is constant and ongoing. While we begin our life free of clutter, rarely does it stay that way. Every moment we are bombarded with information. Some are sediment like distractions — it gathers in the recesses of our mind; we are unaware of its presence until life stirs the sediment. We feel unsettled until we intuitively identify and remove the debris hidden from us.

At other times, the distraction is like a stone that we see and feel. The huge barriers to living intuitively are easy to identify. With practice, we become aware of even the smallest pebbles of distraction. We proactively seek ways to negate distractions and access the extraordinary. We listen to our intuition, filter distractions, and respond to our challenges with increasing accuracy. We move along our intuitive awareness continuum by refining our mosaic.

Intuitive awareness is the refiner of our mosaic. In time and with practice, we recognize even a murmur of a distraction. In that moment, we focus our attention on our mosaic. We move into hyperawareness. We discover the nuances of distraction and what is hiding behind it — our intuitive nudge. Distractions released, we navigate through the triad realities: the mundane, the between, and the extraordinary.

Within the constant bombardment of stimuli, it is difficult to stay focused. When something distractingly attractive tempts us, it takes both courage and practice to stop reacting and focus on our intuition. Recognizing the distraction may be the nudge, we need to reset our intent and claim our intuitive essence. Intent reset, we affirm our intuitive nature and live simultaneously in the triad realities — mundane, extraordinary, between.

No matter where we find our self on the intuitive awareness continuum, we still miss some intuitive cues. While practice may not make us perfect, it does make our connection to our intuition permanent. With a regular practice of resting in the sacred calm and full-body listening, we live in optimal intuitive awareness. Our mosaic is more receptive to the flow of intuition. We miss fewer cues.

Recognizing our intuition requires courage. No matter how long we have been accessing intuition, we may never quite lose the fear of interpreting a nudge wrong. Being intuitive does not mean the absence of fear; rather, it means the acknowledgement of our fears. With this acknowledgement comes courage and humility. We commit to being hyperaware and open to our intuition. We celebrate our inner knowing. In doing so, we effectively circumvent the clutter that becomes increasingly evident in the silence.

Chapter 17

Intuitive Decluttering: From Reaction to Response

We do not live in a vacuum. Our life is a constant kaleidoscope of emotions, thoughts, and actions. We need not be stuck in any subsequent chaos. Listening to our intuition, we navigate through distractions to the core elements of this kaleidoscope. This navigation requires that we intentionally listen to our intuition. Listening, we shift from reacting to distractions to identifying our distractions. This is the first step in responding intuitively.

Intuition vs. Distractions

As we increase our intuitive awareness, we recognize how distractions impair our four aspects: body, mind, spirit, and heart. We learn how distractions contribute to our imbalances. This learning begins with a search for the underlying reasons of the clutter. Then we dig deeper to discover why we attract clutter. We understand that even within clutter are intuitive message that provide growth.

At first, sifting through the material and separating the distractions from intuition may seem daunting and, at times, impossible. As we grow more skilled in filtering distractions from intuition, we become adept in the art of intuitive discernment. As we name our judgments, assumptions, and motives, we gain a greater picture of how each distraction creates illusions that hinder us from recognizing our inner wisdom. This discernment declutters our intuition using deep reflection and introspection.

Discernment is the process of balancing our logical critically thinking mind with our creative self. Through it we discover meaning. It is the foundation of processing our inner wisdom. Through it, we recognize barriers that prevent us from identifying and neutralizing our illusions. We remove barriers that prevent us from living authentically. We recognize that these boundaries are created, in part, by our inability to enter into and maintain sacred calm.

Without sacred calm, distractions overwhelm us. Unable to discern, the connection to our intuitive awareness is broken. We miss our intuitive cues. But, we need not stay in this space. By cultivating clarity, we effectively separate intuitive knowing from illusion. In the sacred calm, our full-body listening realigns our connection to intuition.

Engaged sacred calm brings clarity of life truth. Gaining this clarity does not come without challenges. We may fear what lies at the roots of our thoughts and feelings. Acknowledging fear may prove unsettling. We realize that by confronting what is real, the way we view the world and interact within it changes. We need not be paralyzed by our fears; our intuition guides us through any turmoil into peaceful resolution.

Each time we consciously navigate the turmoil, our intuitive awareness increases. Although it may not be easy, we synaptically prune our fears. We become more resilient. Instead of reacting to distractions and becoming mired in illusion, we return to the sacred calm. Try this: when distracted, breathe deeply to discover what is at the root of your distraction. Be objective about what you find. Instead of rushing to react, feel the distraction, befriend it. Once you are in alignment, intuitively formulate a response.

The Power of Choice

With intuitive awareness comes the power of choice. We can choose to courageously navigate through the clutter or ignore the messages of our intuition. Intuition has the capacity to filter for everything in our life — the truth and the distractions. Even when we commit to moving along the intuitive awareness continuum, the choice of intuition as chief navigator does not create a simple, linear way of life. We ride the thermal of intuition to where it guides us regardless of the path.

As an intuitive, we profoundly feel the clutter — be it old beliefs, habits, or even material items. As clutter is removed from each aspect, additional channels of intuition clear. We live in simple connection. But, living simply in our body, mind, spirit, and heart is not a foregone conclusion; with each discovery of clutter comes the choice to ignore, react, or respond to either intuition or distraction. Each choice lays another tile in the mosaic of our personal reality.

We intuitively create a mosaic of our true self. Woven within our true self is a clutter of beliefs, assumptions, and judgments that are, at the least inaccurate, and, at the worst, untrue. Identifying our illusions provides insight to how our personal reality enhances and weakens our inner wisdom. The truth and illusion of each aspect (body, mind, spirit, heart), once recognized, provide clues to strengthen our authentic reality.

The first step to clearing the path of intuition is naming the illusions within each aspect. This is a step of ongoing self-examination. Next, we acknowledge what paralyzes us. Do not discount the importance of self-compassion. It is a freeing agent that releases us from paralysis and opens us to intuitive engagement. With the practice of self-compassion, we make room for our inner wisdom to flourish.

Instead of struggling against the frenzy in our life, our intuition guides us through it. The noise may not decrease, but our ability to discern our inner knowing increases. We recognize what is diverting our attention. For example: we may find our self in a "loud" environment filled with disconcerting sounds, bright lights or colors, or disparate hot /cold temperatures. We cannot focus; our triggers flip. Entering our sacred calm provides access to resources to recognize the distractions, reset triggers, and move past them.

Through increased intuitive awareness, we gain confidence to discount distractions. We locate and remove obstacles that clutter the gateway to inner knowing. What remains are intuitive messages discerned through anchoring, shielding, and full-body listening. Through discernment, we respond to our inner wisdom with clarity and attend to the world in profound ways.

A distraction presents as clutter in many ways. It might be feelings of unease. It might be an unidentifiable worry or fear. Or, it might be something else. You discover how the distraction manifests for you. This is your intuitive journey. No matter how it manifests, we process it using at least one intelligence. For example: My "go to" for release is using my kinesthetic intelligence. I focus on my breath while moving. I may walk briskly or practice Tai Chi. I clear my mind, enter the sacred calm, and open to what surfaces.

The Perils of Raising Our Energy Vibration

The more we connect to our intuition, the higher our energy vibration. This increased vibration may unanchor us. No longer grounded, our shield is less effective. Our ability to filter distractions is impaired. Our connection is only lost in that moment. When we notice our predicament, we re-anchor and shield reconnecting to our intuition.

If you have difficulty staying grounded, devote time each day to anchoring and shielding. When you are anchored and shielded, consciously engage an intuitive sense facet. Listen to what your intuition says. Then use a specific intelligence to process the information. Use whatever intuitive process you feel is needed in that moment. This practice strengthens the connection between anchoring, shielding, and intuition.

There is no distraction tipping point — meaning you will not be so overwhelmed by your distractions that you will be rendered non-intuitive. There is no intuitive tipping point as well. We do not suddenly become intuitive and no longer get caught by distractions. We will always have distractions and intuitive nudges. Each time we remove clutter, we gain a new level of intuitive response. We become more astute in clearing distractions and gaining insights.

Mindfulness is integral to moving from reaction to response. In the moment, we gain the power to release our distractions while refocusing our intuitive awareness. There is no formula to receiving and processing information. As intuitive change agents, we are open to discovering new ways of receiving and processing while using familiar ways. If we are unclear about what we are receiving, we do not arbitrarily toss out information. We may recognize that only later may we decipher the message. This is perfectly okay.

RI^2 is instrumental in moving from reaction to response. Through it we recognize the roots of a distraction while receiving information about an intuitive message. Through it, we navigate the minefield of distractions (reflection), understand how they weaken our connection to intuition (introspection), and follow a plan created during introspection (integration). We interact through new intuitive patterns of response as we tweak our plans to live with intuitive response.

Intuitive awareness is not an exact science; it requires that we use our resources creatively to access our inner knowing. By decluttering our sacred calm, we access the unique whorls in our intuitive fingerprint. We build upon this knowing as we continue to remove obstacles. The more connected we are to our intuition, the better able we are in navigating and releasing distractions. That is the paradoxical nature of being intuitively aware.

Creating New Pathways of Response

With new patterns of response, we synaptically prune and, in doing so, rid our self of reactionary patterns while reinforcing patterns of response. Synaptic pruning occurs when we develop new habits and ways of responding to the world around us. Our connection to these habits and their subsequent reactions weaken. As this connection lessens, we become more intuitively resilient. With the barriers removed, we create stronger pathways of intuitive awareness.

Two primary ways to create new pathways are to remove distractions or to minimize their impact. Some distractions may be discarded without any impact, but removing a distraction is not always possible. For example: We may not be able to prevent an interaction with a coworker or alter a daily commute.

We minimize the impact of these distractions through our sacred calm. Begin by befriending the distraction to discover why and how it masks our inner knowing. Discern through what trigger the distraction manifests. Learn what challenge is inherent in the distraction. Befriend the distractions. If it cannot be removed, discover ways to manage it intuitively.

As we get more intuitively astute, we maneuver through the minefield created by distractions. Without ongoing discernment, the minefield may seem insurmountable and vast. That is our fear and uncertainty speaking. Intuitively aware, we discover our fears or a lack of understanding of our own power. Through our intuition, our fear minefields are rendered benign. We dismantle barriers to intuitive knowing.

Each time we negate a distraction, our intuitive awareness increases. Our connection to the vast reservoir of intuition deepens. I call this space the Ein Sof. Other names for the Ein Sof are the Great Nothingness or the Void. It has also been referred to as the Quantum, God, the Holy Spirit. Whatever you call this source, our intuitive wisdom flows from this place. No matter what we call it, the Ein Sof is instrumental in accessing our intuition. Each person must discern how this place manifests for them and how they best access it.

Decluttering the Gateway of Intuition

No matter how we gain intuition in the Ein Sof, we must first declutter the gateway. This requires awareness — recognition of our distractions and knowledge of how to remove them. We use our nineteen sense facets and our eight intelligences to remove the clutter. This removal is a precursor to hearing the intuitive message. Note: we need not remove all the clutter to hear our intuition. We remove the clutter that is currently preventing us from engaging our intuition.

The clutter offers opportunities for exploration and discovery as long as we stay in the present moment. Instead of spending time draining our energy through reaction, we enter the clutter through hyper-awareness. Being in the chasm of clutter reminds me of hunting for wild mushrooms. In early spring wild mushrooms hide in plain sight. Shifting our perception, we see a plethora of our wild mushrooms — it is the same for messages of our inner wisdom. We need to move through the obstacles for clear sight.

We cannot force our intuitive awareness or pull knowing from it; rather, we must wait patiently in a state of mindful openness for the message to manifest. As our four aspects align, they resonate with our inner wisdom. This resonance draws intuitive cues to us. Resting in sacred calm, this openness lifts us beyond what we think we know. We do not enter the extraordinary so much as it permeates us. Information gained, we process it in the between and share it in the mundane.

Decluttering distractions is ongoing. This may mean that we declutter what we can while learning to live with other distractions. These remaining distractions can be used to our intuitive advantage. When we know that a distraction is triggered in a given situation, we can shift our paradigm to seeing distractions as colleagues to deciphering intuition.

Moving along the intuitive awareness continuum, we commit to living in the messiness of life while being guided by our intuition. We discover that decluttering is not a separate activity but a way of refining our mosaic and aligning the four aspects of self. Shifting our reactions to responses, we navigate the beauty of the world, clutter and clear, with our intuition.

Chapter 18

The Pause

By now, you have hopefully accepted that you are intuitive. Remember it does not matter where you find yourself along the intuitive awareness continuum; what matters is that you accept your inner wisdom. That is all. That is enough. The degree to which we are intuitively aware depends upon how well we know our self and live from this knowing. We become more intuitively aware as we deepen our knowledge of self; we become more aware of who we are through our intuitive awareness.

Becoming increasingly more intuitive requires synaptic pruning. Through synaptic pruning, we create a network of intuitive pathways. We find ourselves living in greater frequency simultaneously in the triad realities — mundane, extraordinary, and between. Connecting to our inner wisdom along this network, we more easily identify our intuition and decipher it. We become adept in walking amid the worlds and responding to our intuition. The way we perceive shifts until walking amid the triad realities simultaneously becomes our way of life.

Challenges and life lessons are opportunities for conscious growth. As an intuitive, we experience our challenges and life lessons as paving stones of soul purpose. Distractions are experienced as triggers that obscure our intuition. Through the sacred calm, we gain information about what is distracting us and how our intuition is speaking. We are a seeker of truth.

The Pause

Within the sacred calm is the power of the pause. This information gathering moment may be as brief as 5-10 seconds or much longer. We use information gained in the pause to bring our aspects — physical, mental, emotional, spiritual — into alignment. Through this alignment the voices of our intuition increase in volume.

The pause is exactly what it sounds like. We stop. Focus on the moment. Listen to our intuition. During this point of rejuvenation, synaptic pruning occurs. As we connect to intuition firing across our synapses, life unfolds with all its possibilities. By following the path of our intuition, our resilience increases. Instead of having reactions unaware, we transform our reactions into responses.

Longer intentional pauses are necessary to strengthen our connection to intuition. Spending time in quiet, we gain a greater understanding about our self. We learn to sense a trigger and gain the ability to minimize the reaction. During this time, we gain pertinent information about how specific triggers impact us. At times, it is not until after the reaction when we dig into its roots that we are able to explore how our intuition was obscured. Intuitively we learn from our reactions and gain the awareness to respond to future reactions.

Candace Pert, the late Harvard researcher, in her book, Molecules of Emotions, traces the pathway from the triggering of the opiate receptor to the physical sensation of relaxation. This pathway occurs in the space between our emotions and the physical body. Here, emotions trigger sensations that we can measure physiologically. Dr. Pert proved what we have known intuitively for centuries. An intangible stimulus has a great impact on the tangible. This impact impedes our ability to connect to our intuition.

The more intuitively aware we are, the greater our ability to choose response over reaction. Try this: focus on your breath. Don't try to shift it. Notice the space between the inhale and the exhale. Note: you may experience this as a physical place in yourself or it may be a noticing on the spiritual, mental, or emotional plane. Once you become familiar with the nuances of this physical pause, it can be recreated anytime you feel a trigger or need to move into a place of peace.

In the sacred calm of the pause we notice peace fraying. While we may not be able to negate all of the tumultuous impact of the world, we can minimize its roar. Noise reduced; we hear the voice of intuition. Deciphering the intuitive messages, we reconnect with the ethos of peace. Our intuitive awareness thrives within this peace.

An example of how I get caught in reaction: when I am so concerned about getting my point across, I miss signs that tell me an outburst is imminent. If I have fostered sacred calm within the pause, I notice my growing distress and spiking emotions. With this awareness, I have the power to listen to my intuition instead of reacting to my fears.

In the pause is the potential to defuse reactions. With practice, fear is no longer an enemy; rather, it is a reminder of my choice — to react or to respond. Within each moment in pause, I connect to my intuitive awareness and release my need to attach to an outcome, judge others, and defend my position. I grow authentically with each response.

There is nothing magical about the pause. It is a timeless space where intuition percolates. Within it, we have enough time to move from the mundane, gather information in the extraordinary, decipher it in the between, and move back into the mundane to respond. The pause energizes us to live intuitively and responsively in an uncertain world.

Within the pause are seeds of transformation. We listen with our full-body; we reflect and introspect. Full-body listening, reflection, and introspection are necessary to move from reaction to response. Stopping, we reset our attention and formulate a response. Through mindful awareness and intention, we reconnect with our intuitive awareness and act from our compassionate heart.

Maintaining the integrity of our intuitive connection requires incorporating the pause into the whole of our life. In this moment of objective fact-finding, information gained during the pause lays the foundation for connection to our inner wisdom. With practice, the pause becomes a fertile space of intuitive knowing.

Experiencing the Pause

Each of us experiences the pause in our unique way. For example: a friend of mind shared how she responded to a hectic holiday season. Instead of jumping from task to task, she decided to act in the moment. She moved in the flow of her intuitive awareness. After each activity, she paused mindfully. With no set agenda, the next task rose to the surface of her mind. After the holidays, she reported that she was able to ac-

---

complish everything that was important to her while enjoying her family and friends.

Within the pause we are better able to access all nineteen intuitive sense facets and process with our eight intelligences. We engage our Emotional Intelligence by intuitively recognizing even the most subtle imbalance to bring it into alignment. We gain the power to prevent a misalignment before it happens or to bring the four aspects of self back into balance quickly.

The pause bridges the triad realities. Within it, information rises to our consciousness. Without the pause, we may focus on what is distracting. Focusing on the distraction, we get caught in illusion and ignore what is happening. This results in a domino effect of imbalance. For example: I had difficulties in the workplace that triggered imbalances in my mind and emotions. When I fell on black ice, I damaged a disk in my lower spine. My misalignment manifested physically. I was increasingly more emotionally and was unable to communicate effectively.

Pausing in retrospection, I see multiple ways my intuition was speaking to me. I was in a difficult situation at work. Unable to relieve the stressors, they bled over into my other aspects. I did not care for any of my aspects. My body was not the first aspect to suffer misalignment, but it was most certainly the loudest.

Until I was able to bring my physical aspect back into balance, the other three aspects of self continued to be impacted. By caring for the most noticeable misalignment, I was able to use RI2 to assess imbalance in my mind, heart, and spirit. I listened to my internal monologue. I developed strategies to bring them into balance.

The pause increases awareness of our internal monologue, the home of both intuitive cues and distractive illusions. What we sense, intuitive or distractive, can throw us out of balance unless we listen within the sacred calm. Consciously attending to this self-directed conversation reveals intuitive messages and the ways our distractions hijack our intuitive presence.

Pausing gives us the space to stop and regroup. We hear our internal monologue without judgment or defensiveness. Using the information gained, we rescript what we hear before it begins to burrow into other aspects. The pause enables our response. By responding instead of reacting, our intuitive provides spiritual kintsugi in that moment.

Within our emotional body are opportunities for imbalance. This aspect is most often the core domino that triggers during a reaction. Our heart aspect is impacted not only by our emotions but also by the emotions of others that trigger our empathetic nature. Mindfully, we notice if the trigger originated in us or another. We take steps to minimize its impact.

A reaction that appears to have its foundation in a specific situation may only be a flashpoint of a deeper pattern. We may be unaware of the magnitude of our feelings and allow our self to be caught in the emotion. Left unchecked, these misalignments build upon one another. Once trapped by emotions, it takes a significant pause and increased awareness to release the patterns and create a new one.

We all have people in our lives whose energy does not resonate with ours. It seems no matter what is said in a conversation, our emotional equilibrium is disrupted or we disrupt the emotional state of the other. The issue is not that one of us is wrong and the other right. We resonate on different frequencies. This does not make one of us better or another worse. We are just different. This difference makes connection difficult and neurosychrony impossible.

The Pause and The Sacred Calm

Prior to interacting with individuals or groups that hold an incompatible resonance, I spend a significant amount of time in sacred calm. I note how an imbalance manifested previously with the person or group. I describe the manifestation using my five primary senses. If I enter into an interaction armed with sacred calm and the awareness of what prevents me from engaging others intuitively, I am more likely to minimize or even prevent the effects of incompatible resonance. With intuition as my guide, my environment of sacred calm is strengthened.

Our spiritual aspect, although a silent partner, is the primary connector of aspects. This spirit thread weaves through the other three binding them together. We may not notice when the spirit is tumultuous if we do not foster a connection to our divine spark. Through this connection we recognize that an imbalance in another aspect may be an echo of the imbalance in the spiritual aspect.

Our spirit is responsible for this vibrant connection to Sacred and to Earth. By anchoring and shielding we follow the spirit weaving through the other aspects to find frays, fractures, and imbalances.

Unless we actively engage in the cycle of connectivity, our spirit is more likely to move out of balance. The unevenness in our spirit vibrates into each of our other aspects. Our ability to access our intuition is minimized.

Not all our misalignments are gross. An imbalance may be so subtle that we may be unaware until we consciously look for it or the imbalance spikes. During moments of low stress, we may be unable to identify the root cause of what distracts us. In those times, entering the pause and reconnecting with our spirit increases our intuitive awareness.

Regularly entering the pause and evaluating the four aspects help us develop a greater understanding of how these aspects normally interact. Exploring this "normal" provides information about misalignment or find our self in harmony. With daily practice, we are better able to take steps to move into alignment through reframing our thoughts, words, and actions. We become our most optimal, intuitive self.

Enhancing Intuitive Awareness: Connecting the Four Aspects of Self

Connecting body, mind, spirit, and heart is interlocking pieces of a puzzle to create an energized conduit for our intuition. Through this conduit, the volume of intuition is raised. Our intuitive sense facets awaken. Our intelligences are alert. We are alive to the outpouring of intuitive information and pause.

Aligning our body, mind, spirit, and heart begins by resting in the sacred calm, the environment in which the pause occurs. We are drawn to imbalances and discern which aspect holds the core imbalance. If we are unable to know with certainty which aspect holds the primary trigger, we follow the strands of spirit to the heart aspect. If the imbalance is not in the heart, we move to the mind and then the body to search for the core imbalance. We realign each individual aspect and then the whole. With each realignment, our intuitive awareness increases. It becomes easier to find and correct other imbalances.

As an open, aligned conduit, we are filled with harmony and peace. We may experience smoothness, a feeling of joy, or the belief that we can accomplish anything we set out to do. The best way to describe this unity is to use all five of the primary senses. With our eyes we peer into the extraordinary, we hear with clarity, we feel with a greater depth, and we smell and taste the beauty of all.

Once aligned, our world may appear brighter and sharper. Our understanding of sacred calm shifts. For me, within the sacred calm is the flexible, dynamic space where intuitive awareness is enhanced. Within sacred calm, the four aspects interlock to resonate with our intuition. This way of being creates a pause; intuitive response manifests within it.

The interlocking of our body/mind/spirit/heart forms a channel of peace through which compassion and unconditional love flow. Both are vital to deciphering intuitive whispers. When unconditional love and compassion are present, fears and suffering are easily recognized and their barriers more easily breached. Within the pause, we reduce the noise of our fears and increase the volume of our intuition. We respond intuitively.

This process of balancing each individual aspect and aligning our self may seem onerous and time consuming. Necessary to our intuitive awareness, realignment becomes easier with practice. Through this realignment, we recognize wisdom cues. This awareness is rooted in living from our divine spark. Being an intuitive requires that we know our self. Knowing our self is discovering our personal rhythm and shifting into that rhythm in ways that increase receptivity to intuitive nudges.

Chapter 19

Through the Door: Being Intuitive

Awareness is the key that opens the door to our intuition. This door has never been fully closed to us. Its hinges may be rusty from disuse, but at any moment, we can open the door through consciously shifting our perception. One step across the threshold, and voices speak from our intuitive sense facets. Through full-body listening, we identify our intuition.

Once in the extraordinary, we hear the voice of intuition. Information received, we step into the between, where we decipher the intuitive cues and gain understanding. Returning to the mundane, we respond. These are the mechanics of traversing the triad realities to identify, decipher, understand, and respond to intuition.

Creating a Habit of Connection

While we may logically understand the mechanics of moving along the intuitive awareness continuum, creating a habit of connecting to our intuition takes practice. Through this practice, we are forever changed. The way we perceive and experience life radically shifts. Our inner wisdom becomes our internal navigation system. We trust that within our intuition is the power to respond intuitively in an uncertain world.

Each of us has our own unique ways of identifying, deciphering, and fashioning our response to our intuitive cues. In discovering our path, we learn that there is only one extraordinary but many entrances into it. Our journey and the entries into the extraordinary we take are uniquely ours. There is no better or worse place to enter — there is just our place.

No matter where we find our self upon the intuitive awareness continuum, we trust and believe in our innate intuitive abilities. Trust and belief propel us along the continuum. Where we find our self on the intuitive awareness continuum is exactly where we need to be in that moment. As we attune to the flow of intuition, we notice what catches our attention. We recognize that it takes both courage and curious daring to undertake this nonlinear, dynamic journey.

We access our intuition not for another, not for magic, but to reach the fullest potential of soul purpose. As we engage in a3 awareness — awake, alert, and alive — we move between the triad realities gaining information. We enter into a conversation of understanding and then respond intuitively. Integrating our inner wisdom into our lived experience, we evolve into our truest self.

By accessing and responding to our inner wisdom, we grow our ability to collect and process information. As we learn, we engage in synaptic pruning, thus developing a neural network of intuitive awareness. This leads to increased response flexibility. In time, our connection to intuition becomes our primary life guide.

Moving Along the Intuitive Awareness Continuum

No matter how long we have been responding to our intuition, we continue to expand our intuitive awareness by identifying how we access intuitive sense facets and which facets are more difficult to connect to. Recognize that no matter how we choose to move along the intuitive awareness continuum, we start where we are. If you remember nothing about this book, remember that.

For example: I consciously recognize what draws my attention visually when I am alone. Since my intrapersonal intelligence is strongest, I regularly use it to process messages and fashion responses. In order to stretch my abilities, I may use information gained from the same intuitive sense facets but decipher it using another intelligence — perhaps my interpersonal one. My most used intuitive pathways are strengthened while I develop new branches in my intuitive network.

We can and do grow our intuitive abilities in each moment. When aware, we notice the extraordinary shining into the mundane. When we notice our intuition, we can see how the information manifests from other intuitive sense facet. Then, we can use different intelligences to

process the information. We expand intuitive boundaries pushing out the current parameters of intuitive awareness. This means identifying our most easily accessed facets and intelligences.
Walking Amid the Triad Realities

An intuitive does not stop living in the mundane. The mundane is as important as the extraordinary and the between. With increased intuitive awareness, we walk amid the triad realities — moving from the mundane to gain information in the extraordinary and then into the between to decipher the message. Intuition is a guide to interacting and responding to the mundane world while living simultaneously in the extraordinary and the between.

We draw upon our intuition to shift our perception. Unfortunately, we do not always hear or acknowledge the voice of our intuition. We react; our mosaic cracks. This does not sever our connection to intuition. This imperfection, too, is a learning experience. Moving in and out of balance helps us become increasingly more intuitively aware. Through the cracks, our inner wisdom speaks. Listening to our intuition, we undergo spiritual kintsugi. We heal our self through our intuitive response.

An intuitive has the ability to heal the self and the world. Remember, healing is to make whole; cure is a restoration to the original form. We do not provide medical care; rather, we become compassion's presence. This compassion emanates from our body, mind, spirit, and heart. As an emissary of compassion our very presence becomes healing.

A Prescription for Healing

Within our intuition is the prescription for our personal healing. Please understand that we may never be able to cure illness; this does not stop us from healing. This life navigator guides us through our challenges. We identify the roots, decipher challenges, and respond. When we meet challenges, we heal. Each challenge met increases our ability to identify, understand, and respond to our inner wisdom. We live our soul purpose.

Our primary intelligence is the cornerstone from which we explore and experiment with our other intelligences. As we move along the intuitive awareness continuum, we deepen our current skills while gaining new abilities. Creating the foundation through which we process our inner wisdom does not mean that we adopt a narrow or rigid belief of our intuitive awareness. We open to how intuition manifests in our life.

For example: I initially obtained most of my cues when I was alone. As an empath, it was difficult for me, and in some circumstances still is, to filter inner wisdom from distractions when in a crowd of people. Often, after returning home to a quiet solitary space, I recognized the intuitive message that was masked by external and internal noise.

Although it was neither effective nor optimal to respond at this later time, I learned from the experience. I understood that my ability to identify my intuitive cues needed to evolve. I needed to become adept in processing interpersonally. So, I experimented with identifying and processing my intuition in a group. Before entering a group of people, I anchored and shielded. It became easier to process interpersonally. Now, instead of seeing strangers, I see others as part of a welcoming community. I recognize that community presents opportunities to listen to inner wisdom.

On Being an Intuitive Empath

As an empath I am consciously aware of what emotions are mine and what are another's when I am in a group setting. Through this awareness, I objectively separate intuition from distractions. Please note that sometimes I am better able to do this than others. If any of my triggers are activated, I am less likely to filter distractions from intuitive knowing. For me, interpersonal processing is a lifelong challenge.

I realize that to maintain hyperawareness in social settings, I need a strong quiet mind that brings clarity. Initially maintaining hyperawareness while processing interpersonally was exhausting. As I stretched my intuitive muscle, it became easier for me to process with my social intelligence. While it is not one of my stronger intelligences, I am capable of processing intuitive information with it.

The more I process my intuition interpersonally, the greater my ability to shield my empathetic nature while still listening to my intuition in social settings. Now I am no longer so easily distracted in a crowd. I have become an active "engager" in community. I grow increasingly able to be non-attached, non-judgmental — an objective observer. Intuition is my guide.

Developing our intuitive awareness occurs by identifying how intuition presents itself. We return to our intuitive sense facets to discern how they speak to us. We use our intelligences to gain understanding. The more we are able to process this information, the greater our trust in our abilities and confidence in our deciphering.

Becoming an Adept Intuitive

As we grow more adept in identifying, deciphering, understanding, and responding, we learn to use multiple intelligences at the same time. This is the evolution of our intuitive awareness. When we begin to pair one intelligence with others, our ability to hear nuances of intuition deepens. For me, this means pairing interpersonal and kinesthetic intelligence regularly. I might also weave my aural intelligence into the other two to bring clarity to an intuitive message.

There are no rules or successfully tried methods that empower us to process with all our intelligences or enable us to be 100 percent intuitively accurate, 100 percent of the time. Each of our paths is unique. There is no standard formula for embracing our intuitive nature; there is only the one that works for us. As we incorporate other ways of gaining information through our intuitive sense facets and processing, we move along the intuitive awareness continuum.

Opening to our intuitive awareness requires curious daring. We courageously explore the unexpected. When something unusual occurs, we don't ignore it or look for reasons to negate our perception. Instead, we curiously and eagerly explore potential meanings. We dare to believe that our interpretation is true. This stance is imperative to continuing to along the intuitive awareness continuum.

Believing in our abilities requires trust and spontaneity. For example: you may receive an intuitive suggestion to physically change your plans. Perhaps you want to change the coffee shop you are meeting a friend. Or, your intuitive nudges provide information that challenges your beliefs, assumptions, or judgments about a person or situation. Perhaps an insight triggers the recognition and subsequent healing of an old hurt.

As we sync to our inner wisdom, we follow its guidance. We leave the safety of complacency and journey into the unknown. We become more comfortable with the uncertainty inherent in our challenges and lessons. We open to personal transformation and evolve knowing that intuitively powered interactions require flexibility. Being intuitively aware means being courageous in each word, thought, and action.

Intuitively obtained information requires us to shift our perception. We understand the world on deeper, more discerning levels. Our intuition shows us that there is no single way of responding to the world. The more we open intuitively, the more opportunities we have to align our four aspects with our intuition. With these aspects aligned, we live in ways that reflect our soul purpose.

Each moment of awareness is engaged through the 4nons — non-attachment, non-judgment, non-defensiveness, and nonviolence. We are powered by non-attachment by not clinging or pushing away. We let go of any expectation or judgment regarding intuitive messages. With curious daring, we embrace our intuitive nature and open fully without defending or negating the message. We adopt a beginner's mind as we identify, decipher, and respond.

With practice, we travel the triad realties simultaneously. Intuition powers our walk amid worlds. When we are able to connect to our intuitive awareness at will, we are able to identify, decipher, and understand even the most cryptic information. We accept what we know without knowing why or how. The greater our trust, the better able we are to respond intuitively.

This does not mean that we are always able to decipher a message. When we push for absolutes and definitives, the connection to our inner knowing diminishes. In those moments, our defensiveness or violence triggers an obstruction of interpretation. Do not despair. The message is not lost forever. The undecipherable nudges are ways of identifying which aspect is out of balance. They provide opportunities for rebalance and reconnection to our intuitive awareness.

Intuition as a Tool of Self Growth

By connecting to our intuitive nature, we learn more about our self and how we interact with others and the world. Intuition provides us with intangible suggestions for tangible ways to live and interact with others. Our intuitive awareness guides us in the discovery of our true self. It is a transformative force.

We cannot hide from our true self, our agendas, or our illusions once we connect to our intuition. In every moment, our inner wisdom nudges us to be our best, truest self. It does not allow us to accept our illusions as truth. The light of our intuitive awareness burns away the fog of illusion. It becomes increasingly more difficult to live within the illusions while ignoring our insights.

While we may receive sparks of prescience, this is not the primary purpose for our intuition. We are beings who rely upon our intuition to inform and empower our decisions. Intuition is only magical and other-worldly in that it serves as a guide to help us navigate our challenges, provide insights for our life lessons, and facilitate our life purpose. That is the role of our intuition — meeting challenges, learning life lessons, living our soul purpose.

Intuition: The Journey not the Destination

As with many experiences, the road to developing intuitive aware-ness is not straightforward. It is filled with many twists and turns and a detour or twelve. We navigate this road with our internal GPS, our in-tuitive awareness. Even in those moments when we acknowledge that we are lost, we must trust that our intuition guides us onto our life path.

Intuitive awareness is by no means a final destination. Each new ending is merely a resting place after recognizing, identifying, and re-sponding to the intuitive nudge. Each time we integrate our intuition, we gain greater confidence in our ability to connect with and respond to our guidance.

Intuitive nudges and our responses do not occur in a closed circuit. Moving to the rhythm of our intuition widens our community of con-nection. We recognize that we spiral across the clutter in full awareness of the obstacles that prevent intuitive connection. This movement through the clutter is never ending. Each time we complete the circuit through the triad realities, we get better at connecting and responding to our inner wisdom.

With each successive connection to our inner knowing, our intu-itive awareness evolves. Through the transformative force of intuition, we more easily identify when our aspects, individually and collectively, are not in alignment. By bringing the aspects into balance, we move into hyperawareness. Connecting through hyperawareness deepens our connection to intuition through an alignment of our body, mind, spirit, and heart.

Intuition originates in our sacred calm. Within it we recognize the sole purpose of intuitive awareness — to empower us to walk amid the triad realities while integrating these three realities into one. In this triad world, we gain information that enables us to meet challenges, learn life lessons, and live our soul purpose.

Through our intuitive awareness, we take steps to meet our challenges and successfully learn life lessons. We acknowledge that intuition is not just for a certain few...the special. We understand the true purpose of intuitive awareness is to gain knowledge to successfully navigate through our life. We accept that we, and all others, are the special, the intuitive, the chosen.

Afterword

My greatest understanding of the role of intuition in my life is its inherent power as life guide. Through it, we have a power to learn our life lessons, meet our challenges and live with soul purpose. This internal GPS changes everything for us. No longer taking life so personally, we can listen to the messages inherent in each moment and navigate to the place where we need to be. Through intuitive awareness we shift our perception and live in a world made extraordinary.

It has often been said that you write and teach for yourself. Others benefit from the clarity that you gain. So, it is with this book. Through the writing of this book, I gained a better understanding of how I move along the intuitive awareness continuum. With each draft of this book, I understood another nuance of intuitive awareness until I finally said enough. This could have been a book that was written across decades and still I would not have fully explained the hows and whys of intuition. I hope that this stimulates the deepening of your journey with intuition.

I become increasingly more aware of how intuition continues to fully integrate into how I experience the world through my body, mind, spirit, and heart. I am nowhere near the end of the continuum, but I do not despair. I realize that with practice I edge ever closer to listening and responding to my intuition more than I ignore or simply do not hear it.

Two quotes that I have shared throughout this book stay with me. Intuition is magic in that "magic is the art of changing consciousness at will." In order to move throughout the triad realities and create a life of simultaneous integration, we embrace the magic of changing consciousness. "Practice makes permanent" calls each of us to continue the journey no matter how distressed we may be by missed intuitive cues. It gives us hope that intuition is a permanent tool for our journey. Both quotes touch upon the mystery of life and invite us to practice connecting to that mystery. That is the gift that intuition offers us each time we open our eyes and truly see.

The world is an incredible, uncertain place. We navigate through our moments with intuition. What if we listened more often than not and used what we learned to respond to the world? The world would be a much less uncertain, more compassionate place. That is my wish for each of you, individually, and us, collectively. That wish is sent to you on the wings of intuition.

Live each moment in connection with your intuition. That is where transformation sparks.

Vanessa F Hurst
August 2020

Appendix

RI² Process

The RI² Process is a discernment process that connects heart and head, right and left brains. During this process, we assume the stance of objective observer to discern how our intuition is speaking to us. We filter distractions from our intuitive message. In doing so, we identify the roots of our reactions and create ways to move from reaction to response. Using the RI2 Process we meet challenges, learn life lessons, and live with soul purpose.

RI² Process: Reflection

In the first stage, reflection, we hear with the ear of our heart engaging in what I call full-body listening. We listen with all of our senses and to gain information. While we pay attention to the words that we and others utter, we are also aware of nonverbal aspects of our dialogue and any hidden nuances within the message.

Through the ear of our heart we listen, realizing that what is most important is often unspoken. We reflect on what we hear and do not hear; we are open to the deeper, unspoken meanings. We are wide open, courageous, and curiously daring to discover what we do not know. While we might reflect on what we want or do not want, we allow life to show us what we truly need. We open to possibilities that may change us and, in doing so, increase our understanding of life in the present moment.

Non-attachment, the first of the 4nons, non-attachment, non-judgment, non-defensiveness, and nonviolence, is essential to the practice of reflection. It requires us to name what we cling to and those things we are averse to. We surrender. We understand that our perceived reality may not be totally true and accurate. We realize that life is not only about us. No longer do we disregard what is happening to others in the periphery of our existence. We look at life, in the middle and within the margins, impartially and with openness.

Reflection pushes us past our self-imposed limits and invites us to really pay attention—without judgment — to what is being revealed. We intentionally suspend our judgment as we gather information. We acknowledge our beliefs but are not defensive about them. Our goal is to understand how distractions inform our reactions and how intuition informs our responses.

One way to enter and remain in a place of reflection is to attend to the breath. Awareness of our breathing coupled with full-body listening allows us to notice any turmoil that is occurring in our life. Focusing on the breath is the gateway to diving deeply into the reservoir of silence in our quiet mind. Within this space of clarity, our intuitive response dwells. The silent, sacred whispers well up. We hear the message of what is heard, what is seen, what is sensed. When we reflect within our quiet mind using the 4nons, we may be astonished by what our consciousness uncovers.

Engaging in reflection at predetermined moments throughout the day empowers us to practice ongoing reflection in the present moment. If we choose three ten-minute reflection times — in the morning, at noon, and in the evening — we create anchor points of awareness. In time, as we train our minds to engage in reflection, our entire life becomes increasingly one of reflection. Our day infuses with awareness. We connect more fully to our intuition. Practicing reflection becomes second nature.

RI² Process: Introspection

The next step in the RI² process is introspection. While reflection is a way of deepening our awareness of the triggers that inform our reactions and the intuition that informs our responses, introspection helps us to better understand who we are and the roots of our reactions and responses. We discover how we are tripped up by distractions and how intuition is our life guide.

Through introspection we begin to know our self — our uplifting facets as well as our fears and imperfections. The key to introspection is the cultivation of an undefended, non-judgmental attitude. Introspection within the quiet mind activates our intuition in ways that help us to discern how to live more authentically.

Introspection invites us to gain clarity about our intuition. We discern how distractions stop us from living from our intuitive core. During this review or assessment, we look at the bigger picture and see how the pieces have created a whole. Our critical thinking ability and logic are instrumental in understanding how to incorporate an intuitive message into any response.

While practicing introspection, each of us begins exactly where we are in the present moment. Recognizing where we are may be painful. We have spent a lifetime of creating and sustaining life patterns, many of which are not life giving. Perhaps at one time, they helped us to survive. Now we want to make choices that are life giving — ones that help us to thrive. Our intuition provides clues to creating these new life patterns, we have only to be courageous enough to build a life on the foundation of our intuition.

Introspection is the resource through which we understand life patterns and find new opportunities for transformation. Through it, we understand our self and better evaluate what is authentic for us. With that understanding, we are able to recommit to what is beneficial to our life journey and avoid what may no longer work for us or is actually harmful.

With the first step, we engage our inquisitive mind and explore our world with curious daring and without preconceptions. We open to whatever our intuition is saying. We also listen to the voices of distraction. We do not judge our self or our behaviors. With the second step, introspection, we study the whole, both intuition and distractions, and understand their meaning.

During introspection we notice what is preventing us from responding with intuition. We evaluate how those distractions and illusions have impacted our life. We choose how to respond to our intuition in ways that bring transformation.

Practice is everything. Continual reflection and introspection help us to gain a greater understanding of the meanings of our intuitive messages and what is helping or stopping us from moving along the intuitive awareness continuum. Constant and deeper reflection and introspection reveal more intimate, often unacknowledged facets of our self. The material gained from this process can be used to shift fearful reactions to intuitive responses.

RI² Process: Integration

Consciously and unconsciously we choose how we will respond or react to both our intuition and life's unexpected challenges. When we are intuitively aware, our responses are conscious. When we are focused on past regrets or future concerns, we react without self-awareness. Reflection and introspection invite us to be present to those unexpected challenges. When we are mindful and intuitively engaged, we respond out of awareness and understanding. We actively integrate the understanding of our intuitive message that we gain from reflection and introspection. We re-pattern our thinking, align our intent and action, and better engage compassion through our authentic self.

Only through integration of our knowing (reflection) and our understanding (introspection) can true, sustainable transformation occur. Through these two steps, we recognize our intuitive messages and distractions. We better understand our reactions and responses. Integration of the knowing and understanding engages our intent to be agents of compassion. We undergo a paradigm shift. We move along the intuitive awareness continuum and we gain tools to intuitively respond to life's challenges.

Integration is an ongoing opportunity to actively engage our intuitive knowing while diminishing the impact of distractions on our choices. Mindfully aware, we commit to integrating the understanding we gain. We seize every opportunity to respond from our authentic center. We shift away from living through illusions and distractions as we begin to actively and purposefully respond intuitively to our self, to others, and to life. If we are to integrate intuition fully, we must always work to reach a place of understanding. Integrating intuition more fully into our life requires courage and curious daring as we bridge our intent and action.

The 4nons

The 4nons are a mindfulness tool that increases awareness. The 4nons are non-attachment, non-judgment, non-defensive behavior, and non-violence. Through them, we are able to maintain the stance of the objective observer. We filter distractions from intuitive messages and identify, decipher, understand, and respond to our intuition.

- **Non-attachedment**: When we practice nonattachment we are openminded and honest about what hooks us or what we have an aversion to. We understand that to truly engage our intuition, we must objectively experience distractions, without reacting to them when they catch us. We are humble and vulnerable to our intuitive messages. When we are non-attached, we experience distractions in order to understand how and why they hook us. We are open to the many ways our intuition presents. Being non-attached is an objective ongoing shifting of our thoughts, words, and actions in ways that ensure we are not caught by either our distractions or the inability to process an intuitive message.

- **Non-judgment**: We do not judge our abilities or those of another. We do not hold our self as better or more advanced. We open to hearing the truth of our intuition. To be non-judgmental, we must be non-attached. Leaving behind judgment, we open to what our intuition is saying without giving meaning to our distractions. We understand that any internal judgments are to be acknowledged so that they do not take root in the external world and color our ability to neutralize distractions and process intuition.

- No longer defensive, we are humble, modest, and vulnerable to our abilities. Being **non-defensive** means being wide open to what we receive intuitively. We accept that we are intuitive without allowing our abilities to define us. We recognize how an unawareness or denial of our intuition informs illusions and gives strength to our distractions. When our energy is no longer spent defending our self, we no longer need to prove our self.

- The first 3nons are prerequisites to the fourth — **nonviolence**. Objective, without judgment, and non-defensive, we are open to our abilities. We view our inability to decipher a message as a removable barrier. We are gentle, forgiving, and self-compassionate. We use our intuition to strengthen our connection to our core, others, the Sacred, and all of creation.

Full-Body Listening

Full-body listening is a multi-sensory means of engaging the world. Through it, we attend with all of our senses and note how they manifest in our body/mind/spirit/heart. We listen with not only our senses but with the four aspects of our being — body, mind, spirit, and heart. When we listen with all aspects, we notice how our physical body is impacted not only by our senses but by our spirit, emotions, and mind.

We recognize how our body reacts to another's words or action. For example: We may feel our chest tightening in trepidation when harsh words are spoken. We stand straighter when responding to words of praise. Our thoughts and emotions speak through our body in a variety of ways including a muscle twitch and a tickle in our throat.

Full-body listening includes listening to our internal monologue. While our internal monologue might present in words, it is also articulated through emotions, physical feelings, and energetic sensation. Each provides important information. Unless we are attuned to our internal monologue, we miss important information provided by full-body listening.

Using all our senses, we gain impressions and trust that the information we gain helps us formulate the most appropriate response. External full-body listening requires an awareness to our intuitive questions and to distractions that create barriers to the integrating our intuitive messages into our life. We use this information to identify distractions and intuitive messages so that we can decipher, understand and respond to our intuition.

Full-body listening is more than internal and external listening. It is a way of befriending our body. Every time we stop, breathe, and notice the sensations in our body/mind/spirit/heart, we
strengthen the relationship with our self and connect more fully to intuition as guide. We notice aches and pains and discover physical, mental, emotional, and spiritual roots of misalignment. The more we know the four aspects of self, the better prepared we are to respond with compassion.

Full-body listening requires practice. As we become more familiar with our self, the better able we are to discriminate between distractions and intuitive information. With additional practice, we more easily identify our intuition. Our confidence grows; we are poised to decipher, understand, and respond to our intuition. We are better able to navigate our life meeting challenges, learning lessons, and living with soul purpose.

Only through the practice of the 4nons is full-body listening possible. When non-attached, we release the pressure of wanting something to be true or false so badly that we cling to mistruths and push away information that would negate our point of view. Full-body listening requires a non-judgmental, non-defensive stance. Our first instinct may be to judge or defend what we sense. With heightened awareness we trust our body/mind/spirit/heart. We trust our intuition.

When we engage full-body listening, we need not loudly or violently affirm the information we receive. Full-body listening is a tool for strengthening the connection between our intent and action. The more we practice it, the more refined our ability to listen intuitively with all aspects of our body, recognize the nudges, and respond to the messages. Full-body listening is the power behind moving along the intuitive awareness continuum.

Glossary

4 aspects: Each living being, individually and communally, has four aspects. These are the physical body, the mind, the emotional body or heart, and the spirit or energy body. For the purpose of this book they are referred to as the body, mind, heart, and spirit.

4nons: non-attachment, non-judgment, non-defensiveness, and nonviolence: The foundation of a stance that enables us to be objective by not clinging to or pushing something away; acknowledging but not reacting from judgment; understanding our need to defend our self while not acting upon it; being aware of our propensity for internal violence yet acting in peaceful ways.

a3 awareness: awake, alert, and alive: When we are awake, we notice how the extraordinary weaves with the mundane. Being alert is maintaining a state of vigilance. Being alive is the result of being awake and alert. When we are alive we seamlessly integrate our intuitive knowing in our responses.

anchoring: Also called grounding, is a meditative practice that roots us in the moment so that we are hyperaware of our surroundings and better able to listen to our intuition.

bare attention: A process in which our entire attention is focused on the present moment. We are objective and practice the 4nons.

being: A state of hyperawareness in which we connect and act through our soul purpose.

challenge: An exaggerated opportunity to access and use intuition.

clairalience: Intuition draws our attention to odors that provide cues.

clairaudience: Intuitively hearing with clarity the words of another, a song, or our internal monologue. This manifests through many sense facets.

claircognizance: An intuitive knowing without knowing why.

clairgustance: Gaining intuitive cues through our sense of taste.

clairsentience: Physical sensations provide information necessary for us to formulate responses in the world. We intuitively validate the feelings we have in our body.

clairvoyance: This is the intuition of sight. We see the tangible and intangible with our eyes.

compassion spiral: Comprised of three parts — affective empathy during which we feel the emotions of another, cognitive empathy during which we process our feeling and formulate a response, and behavior empathy (compassion) during which we respond.

contemplatio or **contemplation**: Listening quietly to our intuition (part of the intuitive triad).

corpus callosum: A band of nerve fibers connecting the right and left hemispheres of the brain.

cure: Restoration to the original form.

discernment: A process that encourages critical thinking without judging or defending. Through discernment, we discover what is at the root of our actions as well as bring transformation through wide openness.

doing: All of our thoughts and actions. The goal is to have our doing rooted in our being.

distractions: Those things that pull us from the moment and trigger reactions.

emotional intelligence: The ability to identify our emotions and the emotions of others in order to minimize our reactions and respond compassionately.

empathy: The ability to sense the emotions of another.

fishing: Intentionally entering another person's energy field without permission to gain intuitive information.

full-body listening: A means of gathering information both internally and externally through the use of intuitive sense facets.

grounding: Also called anchoring, grounding is a meditation that roots us in the moment so that we are hyperaware of our surroundings and better able to listen to our intuition.

healing: To be made whole.

hyperawareness: A way of seeing the world through intuitive eyes using the practice of a3 awareness. The triad realities merge as the strands of mundane, extraordinary, and between to create our world.

illusion: State of being in which we believe something to be true that is not. This is a result of not being anchored and shielded.

information fatigue: being overwhelmed by the bombardment of both intuition and distractions. When we are fatigued, we mislabel distractions and intuition.

inner wisdom: intuition.

intuition: An inner knowing often manifesting in an "aha" or epiphany moment. When we are connected to it, it serves as our internal GPS.

intuition fatigue: Everything or nothing appears to be an intuitive message. No longer anchored in the moment, our shield no longer protects us from the bombardment of information.

intuitive awareness: The ability to identify, decipher, understand, and respond to inner knowing.

intuitive awareness baseline: The point at which a person finds themselves on the intuitive awareness continuum when they wake to their intuitive abilities.

intuitive awareness continuum: The line that runs from being totally closed to inner wisdom and being completely open to it. We begin at some point along this intangible continuum and move toward wide openness as we increase our awareness.

intuitive equilibrium: Those moments when our four aspects, body/mind/spirit/heart, are aligned, and we are better able to identify, decipher, understand, and respond to our intuition.

intuitive sense: The totality of our sense experience. Instead of having a sixth sense, it is sense comprised of nineteen facets: five primary senses and fourteen additional secondary senses.

intuitive sense processors (IP): Howard Gardner referred to these as intelligences. Through these eight intelligences we process our inner wisdom and respond to it.

intuitive triad: A process of fully listening by focusing our awareness in the moment (meditation), setting our intent to understand (petition), and listening quietly to our intuition (contemplation).

klesha: These mental states of illusion are a direct result of shenpa. They create a barrier that prevents access to intuition

meditatio or **meditation**: Fully listening by focusing our awareness in the moment (part of the intuitive triad)

neural synchrony: A connection of neural pathways between two people. This connection increases their ability to communicate.

neuroplasticity: The ability of the brain to be flexible and evolve in the face of change. Through neuroplasticity we learn new materials at any stage in our life. We can also train ourselves to strengthen our connection to inner wisdom.

objective observer: A person who is aware of their emotions, thoughts, and physical sensations while practicing non-attachment, non-judgment, non-defensiveness, and nonviolence (the 4nons).

oratio or **petition**: Setting our intent to understand our intuitive messages (part of the intuitive triad).

quiet mind: A place of hyperawareness and clarity where intuition can be identified, deciphered, understood, and responded to. The quiet mind is created through the cultivation of silence.

reframing: The ability to find the positive aspects of any situation.

shenpa: What hooks us in our life causing us to react and miss our inner wisdom.

shielding: An energy technique that surrounds us with a membrane of protection that serves as an early warning system for distractions.

silence: More than a cessation of physical noise, this is an environment of clarity. Within silence, we engage full-body listening to discern the difference between intuition and distraction. In this state, we hear with our intuitive sense and understand the message.

soul purpose: The ultimate reason we have incarnated; the culmination of how we respond and react to our challenges and life lessons.

synaptic pruning: Ridding our self of patterns of reactions while reinforcing patterns of response. Synaptic pruning occurs neurally when we develop new habits and ways of responding to the world around us.

triad realities: We live in three different realities — mundane, between, extraordinary. Each has a role in identifying, deciphering, understanding, and responding to our intuition. The mundane has two roles — unaware, this is the reality we find our self in. Once we are awake to our intuition, we respond to it in the mundane. The extraordinary is the place we identify and gather our inner wisdom. In the between, we decipher intuitive messages and formulate responses.

threefold way of access: More than a stance, this is a practice of engagement. Through meditation (meditatio), an intuitive focuses awareness on opportunities to enter the extraordinary and connect to their intuition. Prayer/petition (oratio) is the ongoing petition to understand the intuitive message. Contemplation (contemplatio) is the quiet listening needed to decipher and then respond to intuition.

Works Cited

1. Gardner. H., Frames of Mind: The Theory of Multiple Intelligences (New York: Basic Books, 1983)

2. Frye. T. ed. The Rule of St. Benedict (Collegeville, MN: Liturgical Press, 1981), p. 1.

3. McDonnell, T.P., A Thomas Merton Reader (1996 New York, rev. ed.), Image. p. 387

4. Chödrön, P., Taking the Leap (Boston: Shambhala Press, 2009), p. 22

5. Olsen, K.D. What Brain Research Can Teach About Cutting School Budgets. (Newbury Park, CA: Corwin, 2010), P 2.8

6. Olsen, K., Synergy Transforming America's High Schools Through Integrated Thematic Instruction, (Federal Way, Washington: Kovalik, Susan & Associates, 1995), pp.2-9 – 2.11

7. Goleman, D.,Emotional Intelligence: Why It Can Matter More Than IQ. (New York: Bantam Dell, 1995.)

8. Gardner, H.,Frames of Mind, (New York, NY: Basic Book, 1983.)

9. https://bodytomy.com/corpus-callosum-function Bodytomy June 5, 2019

10. Caponigro, A., The Miracle of the Breath, (Novato, California: New World Library, 2005), pp. 3-14

11. Elkhorne. J. L. Edison, The Fabulous Drone, (72 Magazine,,March

1967), in 73 Vol. XLVI, No. 3 p. 52

13. Caponigro, A., The Miracle of the Breath. (San Francisco, California: New World Library, 2005)

14. Pert. C., Molecules of Emotion, (New York, New York: Simon & Schuster, 1999).

From my Library

I acknowledge those who have inspired me: those who encourage me to experience compassion. Their beliefs and life philosophies have inspired me over my lifetime. Today I stand on a bridge that through their vision and my own now spans my life. Thanks to those who have encouraged me and many others to trust intuition as a guide and life companion. My list is not comprehensive; it is personal.

Bach, Richard, Jonathan Livingston Seagull, (New York: Macmillan, 1970.) Print.

Borysenko, Joan, A Woman's Journey To God, (New York: River head Publishing, 2001.) Print.

Brennan, Barbara, Hands of Light (New York: Bantam Books, 1988.) Print.

Caponigro, Anthony, The Miracle of the Breath, (New York: New World Library, 2010.) Print.

Chödrön, Pema. Comfortable with Uncertainty: 108 Teachings on Cultivating Fearlessness and Compassion, (Boston: Shambhala Publications, 2010.) Print.

---Living Beautifully: with Uncertainty and Change, (Boston: Shambhala Publications, 2012.) Print.

Church, Dawson, The Genie in Your Genes: Epigenetic Medicine and the New Biology of Intention, (Fulton, CA: Elite Books, 2007.) Print.

Cooper, David A., God Is A Verb:Kabbalah and the Practice of Mystical Judaism, (New York: Riverhead Books, 1998.) Print.

---. Seeing Through the Eyes of God, (Boulder: Sounds True, 2007.) Audio CD.

Dennison, Paul E., Brain Gym: Simple Activities for Whole Brain Learn-

158   As Natural As Breathing: Being Intuitive

Douglas-Klotz, Neil, The Sufi Book of Life: 99 Pathways of the Heart for the Modern Dervish, (New York: Penguin, 2005.) Print.

Eden, Donna, Energy Medicine, (New York: Jeremy P. Tarcher, 1998.) Print.

Fry, OSB, Ed., Timothy, The Rule of St. Benedict in English, (Collegeville, MN: The Liturgical Press, 1981.) Print.

Gerber, Richard, Vibrational Medicine, (Santa Fe: Bear & Company, 2006.) Print.

Hahn, Thich Nhat, Peace Is Every Step: The Path of Mindfulness in Everyday Life, (New York: Bantam, 1992.) Print.

Hawkins, David R., Power Vs. Force, (Carlsbad: Hay House, 2002.) Print.

Joy. W. Brugh, Joy's Way, (New York: Tarcher/Putnam. 1979.) Print.

Judith, Anodea, Wheels of Life, (Woodbury, Minnesota: Llewellyn Publications. 2000.) Print.

Kabat-Zinn, Jon, Wherever You Go, There You Are, (New York: Hyperion, 2005.) Print.

Kabat-Zinn, Myla and Kabat-Zinn, Jon, Everyday Blessings: Inner Work of Mindful Parenting, (New York: Hyperion, 1997.) Print.

McCartney, Francesca, Body of Health, (Novato, CA: New World Library. 2005.) Print.

Merton, Thomas, New Seeds of Contemplation, (New York: New Directions Books, 1961.) Print.

---. Raids on the Unspeakable, (New York: New Direction Books, 1966.) Print.

---. Thoughts in Solitude, (New York: Farrar, Strauss, Giroux, 1956.) Print.

Myss, Caroline, Anatomy of the Spirit, (Louisville, Colorado: Sounds True. 1996.) Print.

---. Caroline. Energy Anatomy. (Louisville, Colorado: Sounds True. 1996.) Audio.

Myss, Caroline, and Shealy, Norman, The Science of Medical Intuition:

Self-Diagnosis and Healing with Your Body's Energy Systems, (Boulder: Sounds True, 2002.) Audio CD.

Pert, Candace, Molecules of Emotion, (New York: Simon & Schuster. 1999.) Print.

Rosenberg, M.B., Nonviolent Communication: A Language of Life, (Puddle Encinitas, CA: Dancer Press 2015.) e-book.

Schultz, Mona Lisa, Awakening Intuition, (New York: Three Rivers Press, 1998.) Print.

---. Mona Lisa. The New Feminine Brain: How Women Can Develop Their Inner Strengths, Genius, and Intuition, (New York: Free Press, 2005.) Print.

Seer, Kim, Medical Intuitive Training Level One, (Royal Oak, MI: Seer Holistic Health Services. 2001.) Print.

Seer, Kim, Medical Intuitive Training Level Three, (Royal Oak, MI: Seer Holistic Health Services. 2003.) Print.

Sinnett, Kathy, Energetic Transformations, (Royal Oak, MI: Advanced Energy Works. 2004.) Print.

Silberman, Melvin, PeopleSmart: Developing Your Interpersonal Intelligence, (San Francisco: Berrett-Koehler, 2000.) Print.

Smith, Linda L., Called to Healing, (London: HTSM Press. 2000.) Print.

Soelle, D., The Silent Cry: Mysticism and Resistance, (Minneapolis: Fortress Press, 1997.) e-book.

Stein, Diane, Essential Reiki. (Toronto: The Crossing Press, 1995.) Print.

Weil, Andrew, Spontaneous Healing, (New York: Knopf, 1995.) Print.

Biography

Vanessa F. Hurst is an intuitive-coach-catalyst, author, and artist. She bridges her intuition with her client's. Through increased intuitive awareness, client resolve current challenges, identify life lessons, and live their soul purpose. Vanessa paints aura portraits that reveal life colors and messages embedded in the energy body. She has a master's degree in Natural Health and training in medical intuition, Quantum Healing, Healing Touch, and Reiki. Vanessa nationally presents programs on intuitive awareness, compassion, mindfulness, and contemplative living.

www.ingramcontent.com/pod-product-compliance
Lightning Source LLC
Chambersburg PA
CBHW072142090426
42739CB00013B/3261